KIERKEGAARD
AND THE CONCEPT
OF REVELATION

KIERKEGAARD
AND THE CONCEPT
OF REVELATION

Steven M. Emmanuel

STATE UNIVERSITY OF NEW YORK PRESS

Cover: *Søren Kierkegaard,* by N. C. Kierkegaard, is reprinted courtesy of the Frederiks-borg Museum of National History, Hillerød.

Published by
State University of New York Press, Albany

©1996 State University of New York

For information, address State University of New York Press,
State University Plaza, Albany, NY 12246

Production by Dana Foote
Marketing by Fran Keneston

Library of Congress Cataloging-in-Publication Data

Emmanuel, Steven M.
        Kierkegaard and the concept of revelation / Steven M. Emmanuel.
            p.   cm.
        Includes bibliographical references and index.
        ISBN 0–7914–2697–1 (alk. paper). — ISBN 0–7914–2698–X (pbk. :
        alk. paper)
        1. Kierkegaard, Søren, 1813–1855—Views on revelation.
        2. Revelation.   I. Title.
        B4378.R48E55 1996
        231.7'4'092—dc20   95-30119
                                                                                        CIP

10 9 8 7 6 5 4 3 2 1

Contents

Acknowledgments

I would like, first of all, to express my gratitude to the National Endowment for the Humanities for its generous funding of this project during the final stages of writing, and to Virginia Wesleyan College for its support, and for providing a most congenial environment in which to teach and pursue scholarly research. I would also like to express my appreciation to the staff of the Howard and Edna Hong Kierkegaard Library for their kind assistance, and for making my research stay there so agreeable and productive. A special word of thanks is due to Sumner B. Twiss and C. Stephen Evans for their encouraging support of this project.

Two chapters in this book are slightly modified versions of earlier published articles, reprinted here with the permission of the publishers. Chapter 1 appeared as "Reading Kierkegaard" in *Philosophy Today* (1992), and chapter 3 appeared as "Kierkegaard's Pragmatist Faith" in *Philosophy and Phenomenological Research* (1991). Also, a portion of chapter 6 was originally published in *Religious Studies* (1989) under the title "Kierkegaard on Doctrine: A Post-Modern Interpretation," and is reproduced here with the permission of Cambridge University Press.

Finally, I would like to express heartfelt thanks to my family (on both sides of the Atlantic) for their constant love and support; and most especially to my wife, Henriette, and our sons Daniel, Nicholas, and Marcus. This work is lovingly dedicated to them.

Introduction

In the present study I propose to examine the concept of Christian revelation as conceived in the writings of Kierkegaard. Three primary works have been selected for consideration. Two of these are philosophical inquiries attributed to the pseudonym Johannes Climacus: *Philosophical Fragments* (1844) and *Concluding Unscientific Postscript* (1846). The third work, which was unpublished during Kierkegaard's own lifetime, bears the English title *On Authority and Revelation: The Book on Adler*. Extensive use is also made of Kierkegaard's private journals and papers.

Revelation is without doubt one of the most difficult of theological concepts to explicate. However, it is not my aim to present a fully developed theory of revelation that can stand up to philosophical scrutiny. I am principally concerned with examining the concept of revelation as it is developed in Kierkegaard's philosophical writings, and then only to the extent that it shapes the way he approaches some of the central issues addressed in the authorship. This cannot be done, of course, without placing Kierkegaard's thought within a larger philosophical and theological framework. Indeed, one important outcome of this study is the recognition that Kierkegaard's view of revelation is less akin to the anti-rationalism of modern Protestant theology than has previously been assumed. But the main question that frames this inquiry is the following: what, in Kierkegaard's view, does the Christian concept of revelation, as a suprarational category, tell us about the relation between faith and reason, the relevance of historical knowledge to religious belief, the nature of religious conversion, the concept of truth, the limits of religious authority, and the special form of the religious communication? It is my contention that Kierkegaard presents a coherent and philosophically interesting view of the nature of Christian revelation and, indeed, of the religious form of life that is defined by reference to that central concept.

In the opening chapter, I address the hermeneutic problem posed by Kierkegaard's pseudonymity. On what basis is it possible to determine when the views expressed by the various pseudonyms reflect the mind of Kierkegaard? Commentators have approached this problem in different ways. Recently, numerous attempts have been made to establish Kierkegaard's importance as a forerunner of poststructuralist thought. Those who support this view typically cite Kierkegaard's renunciation of interpretive authority with respect to his own writings, as well as his relentless criticism of all metaphysical attempts to systematize existence. In opposition to such interpretations, I contend that Kierkegaard's understanding of what language is and how it functions is underwritten by the assumption of God's presence; indeed, he assumes that all meaningful forms of communication presuppose real presence. From this perspective, Kierkegaard's aesthetic writings, often cited as evidence against the avowed religious purpose of the authorship, can be seen to take on a new and deeper theological significance than has previously been acknowledged.

In chapter 2, I examine the scope of Kierkegaard's philosophical project and show that the intention in the Climacus writings is to expose a superficial and confused notion of the conceptual qualifications for becoming a Christian. The main target of his attack is Hegel's systematic philosophy, which encourages a false view of the nature of existence and the life of faith. In such a speculative system, faith is reduced to an act of rational comprehension. But by clarifying the Christian concept of revelation, Kierkegaard shows that there can be no objective relationship to God. Faith exists only in the inwardness of subjectivity. The truth that is revealed is not an object for speculative understanding, but for existential appropriation.

Central to Kierkegaard's analysis of revelation is the concept of the "absolute paradox," which is the focus of chapter 3. Against the traditional reading of Kierkegaard, according to which his view of revelation gives rise to an irrationalist conception of faith, I contend that he puts forward a suprarationalist account of revelation, and a pragmatic account of the justification of religious belief. The absolute paradox is interpreted as a conceptual expression for the total incommensurability between an infinite God and a finite human intellect. As such, it signals the impossibility of basing assent to Christianity on theoretical grounds. It does not follow from this, however, that assent is impossible. For where cognitive reason cannot decide the option between belief and unbelief, a decision may be made on practical grounds. Kierkegaard distinguishes between probative rationality, which is based on evidential reasons, and pragmatic rationality, which is based on practical reasons. The paradox forces the realization that the justification for accepting the Christian revelation must finally be made on practical and ethical grounds. It is in this context that I interpret the role of sin-consciousness in the decision to believe.

Next, I examine the consequences of the absolute paradox for Kierkegaard's understanding of the relation between faith and history. On the one hand, he recognizes the necessity of the historical manifestation of God as prerequisite for faith and salvation. Yet he also recognizes that a natural concern for historical accuracy may come into direct conflict with the requirements of obedient discipleship. Although a historical point of departure is necessary for faith, historical inquiry is at best inconclusive and at worst positively harmful. It has been argued that although evidential considerations are neither necessary nor sufficient to produce faith, they may well play an important role in confirming an existing faith. I contend that this line of criticism underestimates the extent to which Kierkegaard's discussion is framed by the theological concept of obedience.

In chapter 5, I explore the relation between grace and will in the transition to Christian faith. The current debate divides scholars broadly into two camps. Some argue that divine grace is the central feature of Kierkegaardian faith, and hence they deny the efficacy of human activity in conversion, while others emphasize his remarks concerning the constitutive role of the will in coming to believe, and even criticize him for advocating an untenable form of volitionalism. Taking my point of departure from recent work by M. Jamie Ferreira and others, I propose an interpretation which attempts to mediate between volitionalist and antivolitionalist accounts.

The essentially subjective nature of Kierkegaardian faith raises a further question about the function of Christian doctrine in the religious life. In contrast to a 'propositional' view, which says that doctrines function chiefly as informative statements or truth claims about objective realities, Kierkegaard appears to have regarded doctrines primarily as rules for regulating the speech and action of the religious community. In this respect, his view is formally similar to the regulative theory of doctrine recently proposed by George Lindbeck. In chapter 6, I attempt to show that the salient features of the regulative theory are anticipated in Kierkegaard's analysis of subjectivity and religious truth.

Even though the emphasis in the Climacus writings is on subjectivity and inwardness, Kierkegaard does not endorse the view that Christian truth is a purely arbitrary matter. The discussion of doctrine makes it clear that true religious subjectivity must conform to the objective standard that is set by the Christ-revelation. The life of the believer must be regulated in all its aspects by reference to dogmatic Christian concepts. This point is crucial to understanding the full import of Kierkegaard's critique of Christendom and Christian speculation. For as we discover in *On Authority and Revelation*, the most serious problem posed by the influence of speculative philosophy is not merely that it encourages an objective relationship to doctrine, but that it volatilizes the language of Christian theology, and thereby threatens to make it impossible for individuals to be properly related to the object of Christian faith.

In *On Authority and Revelation* Kierkegaard examines the case of Adler, a Hegelian pastor of the Danish church, who claimed to have received a revelation from Jesus Christ. The originating concern of this work, which is the subject of chapter 7, is reflected in the following question: How far may a person be justified in asserting that he has had a revelation? Arguing *e concessis*, Kierkegaard shows that Adler lacks the conceptual understanding required to assert that anything could count as a revelation in the Christian sense. It is further shown that his religious confusion stems precisely from the fact that he has a speculative understanding of Christian concepts. He is so thoroughly imbued with Hegelian ideas that there is no hope that he could understand himself in relation to his claim to revelation. Adler is thus held up as a satire on Hegelian philosophy and an epigram upon Christendom.

It is surprising how little attention the book on Adler has received in the secondary literature. Synoptic studies of Kierkegaard's thought typically treat it as a minor work, which at best marks a transitional phase in the development of Kierkegaard's polemic against the established church.[1] It is my contention, however, that commentators have underestimated the intrinsic importance of this book for understanding Kierkegaard's overall philosophical project. For a closer examination shows that the book on Adler is not only deeply rooted in the conceptual universe of the *Fragments* and *Postscript*, but it is also an extension of the analysis of Christian revelation presented in those works. Moreover, by focusing as it does on the formal structure of Christianity, on the objective content of its doctrines, this book may be seen as a completion of the earlier analysis.

In the final chapter, I examine Kierkegaard's theory of indirect communication. Working mainly from his 1847 notes for two lectures on communication, I attempt to show how this theory ties in with the major themes developed in the authorship, and more important, how it shapes his understanding of the Christian incarnation, which itself represents an indirect form of communication. This is followed by a brief concluding section, in which it is suggested that Kierkegaard's analysis of reason, faith, and revelation may provide a useful model for understanding the relation between philosophy and theology.

1

Revelations of Self
in the Pseudonymous Authorship

Between 1843 and 1846 an extraordinary series of pseudonymous works from the pen of Søren Kierkegaard appeared in the bookshops of Copenhagen. The series began in February 1843 with the massive two-volume set *Either/Or*, edited and annotated by Victor Eremita. This was followed eight months later by the simultaneous appearance of two shorter works: *Fear and Trembling*, by Johannes de Silentio, and *Repetition*, by Constantin Constantius. In June 1844 came three more slender volumes: *Philosophical Fragments*, by Johannes Climacus, *The Concept of Anxiety*, by Vigilius Haufniensis, and *Prefaces*, by Nicolaus Notabene. The series was rounded off with the publication of two substantial works: *Stages on Life's Way*, which appeared in the spring of 1845 under the editorship of Hilarius Bookbinder, and Johannes Climacus's *Concluding Unscientific Postscript to the Philosophical Fragments*, which appeared in February of the following year.

As if to accentuate the pseudonymous nature of these books, Kierkegaard published under his own name a concurrent series of devotional writings intended for "edification."[1] Collectively, these pseudonymous books and edifying discourses comprise what Kierkegaard would later refer to as his "authorship," though in truth they account for only part of the total literary production, which continued until shortly before his death in 1855.

Kierkegaard's professed intention in employing pseudonyms was twofold: first, to present the reader with a choice between a number of competing world views or existential possibilities; and second, to withdraw himself from the process of interpretation by presenting these views in such a way that the reader would be free to make a personal decision.

However, the very same strategy by which Kierkegaard sought to educate and liberate his readers, today poses a formidable challenge to the exegete, whose purpose it is to interpret Kierkegaard's meaning. For on what basis is it possible to determine when the views expressed by the various pseudonyms reflect the mind of Kierkegaard? Commentators have approached this question in different ways. In this chapter I shall examine a variety of what may be characterized as "modern" and "postmodern" responses to the problem of reading Kierkegaard.

THE PROBLEM OF KIERKEGAARD'S PSEUDONYMITY

Traditionally, literary critics have tried to get a handle on the meaning of a text by tying it into the author's creative intention. But Kierkegaard's pseudonymous authorship, with its elaborate system of Chinese boxes, proves to be an especially frustrating subject for intentionalists. In *Either/Or*, the papers of several fictional authors are brought to light by a fictional editor; in *Repetition,* the young man with whom Constantin corresponds turns out to be no more than a psychological experiment, a product of Constantin's imagination; and in the *Postscript,* Climacus reviews the work of other pseudonyms, thus creating an internal structure of reading and criticism. Perhaps the most striking example of this strategy of mystification is the provocative article entitled "Who is the Author of *Either/Or?*", ostensibly written by a pseudonym whose own papers appear in the first volume of that work.[2]

In "A First and Last Declaration," which we find appended to the *Postscript,* Kierkegaard explains that his relationship to the pseudonyms is more tenuous than that of an author who merely creates fictional characters. "I am," he writes, "impersonal, or am personal in the third person, a *souffleur* who has poetically produced authors, whose prefaces in turn are their own production, as are even their own names."[3] As Bertel Pederson points out, Kierkegaard does not see himself as the powerful director behind the scenes, but as one who at most assists or prompts the "authors" to perform. At every turn, the pseudonyms undermine Kierkegaard's authority over the texts.[4]

Commentators have attempted to circumvent this problem in two characteristic ways. On the one hand, the unusual richness and intensity of Kierkegaard's life has drawn the attention of scholars in search of an interpretive key to his writings. This tendency has been fostered in part by a long and respected tradition in Kierkegaard studies which is straightforwardly biographical in orientation.[5] The primary object of this type of inquiry is not the text itself, but Kierkegaard's personal life and the historical context in which he lived and wrote. The biographer probes into Kierkegaard's letters, papers, and diaries, in an attempt to penetrate his innermost thoughts and feelings, to reveal the man behind the masks.

Kierkegaard, who consciously wrote from his personal experiences, was well aware that many of his readers would try to identify him with the pseudonyms, and he actively sought to preempt such readings. In "A First and Last Declaration," he explicitly warns us against attributing to him any of the statements found in the pseudonymous works. He claims that he is no closer to any one pseudonym, but equally far from them all; that it is foolish to bring his biography into the discussion as if that could shed light on anything, least of all the true significance of the authorship. In this, Kierkegaard seems to have anticipated a view that would become commonplace in twentieth-century literary criticism.

Other commentators, myself included, have attempted to focus specifically on the philosophical content of Kierkegaard's writings. As C. Stephen Evans explains, "If we are interested in the truth of the views presented . . . then it really does not matter very much whether Kierkegaard personally held these views. For from the fact that he held a view, nothing follows as to the truth, profundity, or value of the view."[6] Although historians and biographers will have a valid interest in the question of how Kierkegaard stands in relation to his pseudonyms, this is not properly a philosophical concern.

The philosophical approach to interpreting Kierkegaard tries to avoid the problem created by the pseudonyms by shifting the focus of inquiry to a purportedly neutral ground. However, if we find in Climacus an argument to the effect that faith is not a species of knowledge, we may still wish to ask how Kierkegaard stands in relation to that particular argument, or what he is trying to accomplish with it, if anything. Even if the truth, profundity, and value of the argument is independent of Kierkegaard, we may still wish to know how it is to be interpreted within the larger context of his literary production. This type of inquiry forces us to go beyond the point of view of any single pseudonymous author. To claim that we should be concerned only with the pseudonyms or their arguments is merely to defer the problem of reading, which resurfaces as soon as we consider the authorship as a totality.[7]

Kierkegaard addresses this problem of reading in two autobiographical works, *My Activity as a Writer* (1851) and *The Point of View for My Work as as Author* (written in 1848, published posthumously in 1859). In the latter, Kierkegaard explains that he was essentially a religious author, and that his writings were designed to throw light on the problem of becoming a Christian.[8] He admits that he was not absolutely clear about this task from the very beginning, but that the failure of the aesthetic life to provide a satisfactory answer to his deepest existential concerns forced him to the realization that an answer could be found only in religious categories. Furthermore, he suggests that the hand of Providence was guiding his progress in this direction, enabling him to produce a literature that served to illuminate the true nature of the religious life.[9]

But Kierkegaard's explanation seems to invite as many questions as it answers. One wonders, for instance, why a religious writer would employ aesthetic means to achieve a religious end. This question is directly addressed by Kierkegaard in Part One of *The Point of View.*[10] There it is explained that the religious purpose of the authorship was to dispel the "monstrous illusion" of Christendom: the fact that his contemporaries had come to regard themselves as Christian as a matter of course, despite the fact that they lived their lives in aesthetic categories. Believing that a direct attack would only cause people to cling all the more tightly to this illusion, Kierkegaard reasoned that indirect tactics were required: "If it is an illusion that all are Christians—and if there is anything to be done about it, it must be done indirectly, not by one who vociferously proclaims himself an extraordinary Christian, but by one who, better instructed, is ready to declare that he is not a Christian at all."[11] Kierkegaard thus sought to win the sympathy of his audience by provisionally adopting an aesthetic point of view.[12] Having thereby opened a line of communication, he could proceed to illustrate the poverty of the aesthetic life, and so place his readers in a position to realize for themselves that they were not living in accordance with the requirements of true Christianity.

Kierkegaard acknowledges that the indirect strategy employed in the pseudonymous works is a form of deception. However, he urges us not to be alarmed by the word 'deception.' For, as he points out, it is not only legitimate to deceive a person for the sake of the truth, but also to deceive a person *into* the truth.[13] The deception, of course, lies in the fact that Kierkegaard does not begin *directly* with the religious, but engages in diversionary tactics in order to get to the religious point of view. He contends, however, that precisely this form of deception was required to dispel the illusion of Christendom.[14]

Commentators have generally accepted this post-pseudonymous explanation at face value, pointing out that it establishes a normative framework for interpreting the authorship. According to Paul L. Holmer, a work like *The Point of View* provides the reader with a "logical" standpoint from which to judge the meaning and validity of the entire aesthetic production.[15] C. Stephen Evans seems to concur, observing that it is in fact not hard to show that "a good many of the opinions expressed by the pseudonyms were held by Kierkegaard himself. The method whereby this can be done is simply to compare the pseudonymous works with the works that Kierkegaard wrote under his own name and with his opinions as expressed in his *Journals and Papers*."[16] In this way the writings that appear under Kierkegaard's own name are seen as establishing a natural ordering of the texts.

But if we take seriously the alterity of the pseudonymous texts–the position that Kierkegaard could only discuss these texts from an external standpoint (the position he claimed for himself in 1846)–then how are we to understand a book that claims to offer us *the* point of view for the authorship? It would seem that such a book oversteps the limitations already imposed on what can be said. At the very least it invites our suspicion concerning the author's true motivation for writing it. This situation has prompted some commentators to insist that the distinction between truth and fiction in the authorship cannot be decided merely by reference to Kierkegaard, whose own writing serves only to complicate the relation between the writing self and the written word.

In a penetrating study of the primary documents, Henning Fenger challenges Kierkegaard's claim that a religious element was present in the authorship from the very beginning.[17] Fenger offers evidence of a systematic attempt on Kierkegaard's part to suppress, misrepresent, and deliberately falsify documents pertinent to the interpretation of his life and works. The central thesis of his book is that "Kierkegaard-research went down the wrong track at the outset and that 'the mistake,' to a certain extent–to a great extent–goes back to Kierkegaard himself" (xiii).

The implicit assumption guiding Fenger's study is that, although we cannot trust Kierkegaard's own claims concerning his purpose in the authorship, we can approach the truth of the matter by checking these claims against external sources. Judging from the sources, it appears that the real motivation behind Kierkegaard's aesthetic production was not religious at all, but the fact that he failed to win acceptance by the elite literary circle of his day. Fenger contends that Kierkegaard's authorship grew out of his profound resentment against this intellectual coterie, and more specifically against its *arbiter elegantiarum*, Johan Ludwig Heiberg, for failing to acknowledge his literary genius. The subsequent attack on Hegel and romanticism is thus seen as a direct result of the conflict with Heiberg and not, as Kierkegaard would later have us believe, an abiding religious concern to clarify the requirements of Christian faith.

Fenger argues convincingly that many of the private writings, including the famous Gilleleje notation from the spring of 1838 (which scholars have taken as a record of Kierkegaard's religious conversion), are not autobiographical in nature, but rather the remnants of an abandoned literary project (81-135). This type of error could simply be attributed to the careless treatment of primary documents. However, the "myths" Kierkegaard created about himself, his authorship, and his relationships to key people in his life, are much more difficult to trace. Fenger presents evidence of Kierkegaard's early romantic attachment to a young woman by the name of Bolette Rørdam; a relationship that predated his engagement to Regine Olsen, and which he later attempted to conceal from posterity (150-157). Moreover, in sharp contrast with Kierkegaard's own account of the momentous break with Regine, Fenger maintains that the real crisis was precipitated when Kierkegaard learned of Regine's subsequent engagement to another man. From this standpoint, Fenger writes, "it is altogether understandable that he now leaps into faith and glorifies his 'sacrifice': his renunciation of Regine becomes a religious act in the service of higher powers" (219).

According to Fenger, Kierkegaard had established himself as an aesthetician with the publication of *Either/Or* in 1843, and from that time on he could not legitimately ask to be taken seriously as a religious writer (2). The story of his early conversion to Christianity and of the great personal sacrifice he endured to become a writer in the service of his faith are merely examples of the way Kierkegaard poetically transformed his life into literature.

Commenting on Nietzsche's aestheticism, Alexander Nehamas writes:

> Nietzsche . . . looks at the world in general as if it were a sort of artwork; in particular, he looks at it as if it were a literary text. And he arrives at many of his views of the world and the things within it, including his views of human beings, by generalizing to them ideas and principles that apply intuitively to the literary situation, to the creation and interpretation of literary texts and characters.[18]

These words could with equal justification have been written about Kierkegaard, whose pseudonyms dramatize the relation between the aesthetic, ethical, and religious forms of life. But whereas Nehamas discerns in Nietzsche's aestheticism a strategy for developing the thesis of perspectivism, Fenger contends that Kierkegaard had no clear sense of the boundary between fiction and truth, illusion and reality.[19] His life must be regarded as "a gigantic play in which [he] acted a profusion of roles, among them that of Søren Kierkegaard in countless versions."[20] If there is a clear moral to be drawn from all this, it is the following: that where literal truth is concerned, we are no better off looking to Kierkegaard's later writings than to the earlier pseudonymous ones.

There are, however, a number of problems with Fenger's argument. First of all, he does not fully acknowledge Kierkegaard's own repeated assertion that the religious reason behind his use of the pseudonyms was neither dominant nor decisive when the aesthetic project was begun. In *My Activity as a Writer*, Kierkegaard confides: "So it is that I understand everything *now*. From the beginning I could not thus survey what has been in fact my own development."[21] Fenger's failure to grasp this point gives rise to a curious tension in his argument. For, on the one hand, he wants to claim that Kierkegaard was merely a "poetic" Christian; yet he does not want to rule out the possibility that Kierkegaard at some point sincerely committed himself to Christian faith. But in this case, as George Stack points out, it is really only a question of timing, not one of truth.[22]

Fenger's argument is further weakened by the fact that it does not adequately account for the eighteen "edifying discourses" Kierkegaard published between 1843 and 1844. These devotional works, which form a common thread running throughout the literary production, pose a serious challenge to the claim that there was no clear religious element present in the authorship from the start. The first two discourses, "The Expectancy of Faith" and "Every Good and Every Perfect Gift is From Above," appear shortly after the publication of *Either/Or*. Fenger acknowledges this fact, hastening to add that the majority of Kierkegaard's early writings, including those published prior to *Either/Or*,[23] belong to the category of the aesthetic. But he does not explain how the discourses fit the aesthetic pattern of these early writings, nor does he suggest what purpose they might otherwise have served. Fenger does note, in passing, that Kierkegaard waited until May 1843 to publish the aforementioned discourses, and he wonders whether it would not have been more consistent with the religious aim of the authorship to have published them simultaneously with *Either/Or*.[24] However, in view of the fact that these works are separated by less than three months, Fenger's objection does not appear to be a very serious one.

Furthermore, it may be noted that *Either/Or* was quickly followed into print by a series of articles, all designed to draw attention to the peculiar form and content of the larger work. I have already mentioned one of these in passing.[25] The others include an ironic piece by Victor Eremita entitled "A Word of Thanks to Professor Heiberg," in which the author replies to Heiberg's hastily prepared review of his book; and an article by Kierkegaard entitled "A Little Explanation," in which he disputes the "persistent rumor" that the sermon which concludes *Either/Or* is in fact the same sermon he once preached as a student in the pastoral seminary. The latter article was published on May 16, the same day as *Two Edifying Discourses*. Thus, *Either/Or* was very much a fresh topic of discussion when the first discourses quietly appeared on the scene; and this fact is in every way compatible with the indirect strategy Kierkegaard describes in *The Point of View*.

A third and far more serious problem, however, concerns the scope of Fenger's work. As a source critic, Fenger is perfectly within his rights to attempt to construct a picture of Kierkegaard in the social and historical context of Golden Age Denmark. Yet it seems that he wants to do more than this. For the thesis of his book is not merely that we have misunderstood the early influences on Kierkegaard's life, but that as a direct result we have misinterpreted the authorship. In this way, the distinction between the man and the text is subtly dissolved; Kierkegaard's life becomes the basis for interpreting his work.

However, it is a more or less received opinion among literary theorists that, regardless of what we may know about an author's life, it is a mistake to suppose that textual meaning is grounded in authorial intent. This view questions the suspicion that there must always be a deeper fact about what a text really means; that deep in the mind of the author at the moment of creation there lies a clue that definitely settles the issue of correct interpretation. It is precisely this suspicion that Wimsatt and Beardsley have called the "intentional fallacy."

Following this line of criticism, I would argue that Kierkegaard's intention is neither available nor desirable as a standard for judging the meaning or the value of his authorship. This is not to say that there is no room for biography in textual interpretation, but rather that biographical considerations, being external to the text, must always be regulated by the philological constraints presented by the text itself. The closest we can ever get to Kierkegaard's intending mind, outside his texts, will still be short of his effective intention as this appears in the texts and can be read from them. True, we must admit the possibility that Kierkegaard's retrospective interpretation of the authorship plays fast and loose with the facts. What is really interesting, however, is not that he asks us to read the authorship that way, but that it *can* be read that way. Kierkegaard's truthfulness is only an issue if we assume that textual meaning is identical with authorial meaning, or that a text must mean what an author says it means.

More interesting still is the fact that this view of textual meaning is largely anticipated in the pseudonymous writings. The article "Who is the Author of *Either/Or?*" pokes fun at the view that knowledge of an author's identity is indispensable to a proper appreciation of his work. The piece concludes with the following observation: "Most people, including the author of this article, think it is not worth the trouble to be concerned about who the author is. They are happy not to know his identity, for then they have only the book to deal with, without being bothered or distracted by his personality."[26] And several years later, in a section of the *Postscript* entitled "A Glance at a Contemporary Effort in Danish Literature," Climacus comments:

> Whether my interpretation is the same as that of the authors, I can of course not know with certainty, since I am only a reader; on the other hand, it gives me pleasure to see that the pseudonyms . . . have themselves said nothing, nor misused a preface to assume an official attitude toward the production, as if an author were in a purely legal sense the best interpreter of his own words; or as if it could help a reader that an author had intended this or that, if it was not realized; or as if it were certain that it was realized because the author himself says so in the preface.[27]

Here, Kierkegaard's most developed pseudonym directly challenges the assumption that knowledge of the author's creative intention is indispensable to the activity of textual interpretation. And in the very same breath he suggests what he takes to be the correct critical stance for an author to take toward his own work, namely, that of a reader.

But what scholars have tended to overlook is the fact that when Kierkegaard comments on his relationship to the pseudonymous production he maintains the very same position. In "A First and Last Declaration," for example, Kierkegaard explicitly disavows interpretive authority over the pseudonymous texts by reducing his status to that of a reader. As he writes: "I have no opinion regarding [the pseudonymous books] except as a third person, no knowledge of their meaning except as a reader, not the remotest private relationship to them, since this is impossible in a doubly-reflected communication."[28] This position is later reaffirmed in the autobiographical works. In *My Activity as a Writer*, we read: "That I was 'without authority' I have from the first moment asserted clearly and repeated as a stereotyped phrase. I regarded myself preferably as a *reader* of the books, not as the *author*."[29] And again, in Part One of *The Point of View*, where Kierkegaard explains that he was essentially a religious author, he writes:

> It might seem that a mere protestation to this effect on the part of the author himself would be more than enough; for surely he knows best what is meant. For my part, however, I have little confidence in protestations with respect to literary productions and am inclined to take an objective view of my own works. If as a third person, in the role of a reader, I cannot substantiate the fact that what I affirm is so, it would not occur to me to wish to win a cause which I regard as lost. If I were to begin *qua* author to protest, I might easily bring to confusion the whole work, which from first to last is dialectical.[30]

Kierkegaard acknowledges that, as a historical person and efficient cause of a literary text, one is naturally compelled to think that one's own interpretation is the correct one and to proclaim it as such; and that if one is a religious writer, one may feel that one has a duty to insist that the work be read that way. But as an *author*, Kierkegaard readily admits that it does not avail much that one intends this or that.[31] By bringing a text into the public domain the author relinquishes all authority over what it means; the text assumes a life of its own. Now the only interpretation that is entitled to be called correct is that which can be demonstrated on the basis of the text.[32]

In line with the theoretical assumptions of the New Criticism, Kierkegaard holds that statements of authorial intention are in a sense irrelevant because, if the intention can be found in or inferred from the text itself, the statement is superfluous, and if the intention cannot be found in or inferred from the text, the statement is to no avail. This claim rests on an implicit distinction between literary and nonliterary modes of expression. Kierkegaard does not claim that his literary texts do not mean what he intends or understands them to mean; rather he claims that their meaning cannot be judged solely on the basis of his nonliterary statements about them. This is entirely consistent with Kierkegaard's view of himself, *qua* critic, as a reader of the authorship.

It should be clear from the foregoing that Kierkegaard does not begin by disavowing interpretive authority over his texts only to reclaim this privilege in his later writings. Kierkegaard's "point of view" is to be understood as one possible perspective, which the reader may either accept or reject based on his own encounter with the texts. Kierkegaard merely exercises a right reserved by every author, namely, to offer his own interpretation of his work. It follows that a book like *The Point of View* might well suggest a promising way of reading the authorship, whether or not the account it presents can be shown to be "authoritative." For the salient question is not whether Kierkegaard was, as a matter of fact, an author in the service of Christianity, but whether that account of his purpose is corroborated by the texts. From this standpoint, one could argue that the received interpretation of the pseudonymous authorship is still the best and most comprehensive available.

Thirty years ago this interpretation of Kierkegaard would have placed him in the mainstream of literary criticism in America. Since then, however, the New Criticism has gradually faded into the background, and in its place we have seen the steady rise of Deconstructive Criticism and another nineteenth-century philosopher, Friedrich Nietzsche. Deconstructionists, inspired by Nietzsche's views on reading and textuality, have gone far beyond the formalist attempt to deny authors any special interpretive privilege. By challenging our basic ideas about what a text is, these poststructuralist critics have articulated the problem of reading at a deeper level.

Recently a number of scholars have attempted to resurrect Kierkegaard, too, by proclaiming him a forerunner of the kind of critical work now being done in the postmodern tradition.[33] These commentators have produced highly original and provocative readings of Kierkegaard's texts. Yet there is one common premise that shapes their critical outlook: That the Derridean critique of the metaphysics of presence, on which the deconstructionist project rests, is essentially correct, and that Kierkegaard may be regarded as an early critic of presence. This claim must be examined more closely.

KIERKEGAARD AND DECONSTRUCTION

The word "presence," as it is used by Derrida and others, refers to a foundational or self-certifying ground outside of language which guarantees the meaningfulness of utterances within language. As Jonathan Culler explains:

> The notions of "making clear," "grasping," "demonstrating," "revealing," and "showing what is the case" all invoke presence. To claim, as in the Cartesian *cogito*, that the "I" resists radical doubt because it is present to itself in the act of thinking or doubting is one sort of appeal to presence. Another is the notion that the meaning of an utterance is what is present to the consciousness of the speaker, what he or she "has in mind" at the moment of the utterance.[34]

In opposition to this tendency, Derrida maintains that signs get their meaning not from some extralinguistic reality which they signify, but by virtue of the relations they bear to other signs in the linguistic system.[35] Following Saussure, Derrida conceives of language as a differential system of signs. The signifier "cat" is what it is not because it is directly related to a particular signified, but because it is distinct from other words in the system, such as "mat" and "cad." The word "cat" is thus inhabited, both phonically and graphically, by the traces of forms one is not uttering, and it can function as a signifier only in so far as it contains these formal traces.

Because the meaning of a sign is differentially defined in terms of what it is not, rather than in terms of some positive relation (e.g. correspondence), its meaning is always in some sense absent from it. Yet, our invincible tendency as competent users of language is to assume that our own meaning can be made present to others; if not in the act of writing, then certainly in the act of speaking. This is reflected in Saussure's contention that writing is derived from, and hence secondary to, speech. But, as Derrida points out, this privileging of the spoken word merely gives rise to the illusion of the full presence and unity of meaning in the spoken word. Indeed, the assumption of presence characteristic of the history of Western philosophy and linguistics is perpetuated by this "phonocentric" bias, which in turn gives rise to the general tendency to make certain terms more dominant than others in language.[36]

Contrary to traditional semantic theories, Derrida maintains that meaning is not immediately present in any one sign, but is the effect of a potentially endless play of signification. The differences between signs account for the apparent specificity of their significations, and hence for the possibility of intelligible communication. But because these significations can never come to rest in an absolute presence, we are propelled into an endless regress of meaning. When we look up the meaning of a word in a dictionary, we find a lexicographer's definition. But a lexicographer, as Quine has pointed out, is an empirical scientist, whose business is merely the recording of the meaning speakers have given words in the past.[37] And, as Culler notes, "what is true of a word is true of language in general: the structure of a language, its system of norms and regularities, is a product of events, the result of prior speech acts. But once we take this argument seriously and begin to look at the events which are said to determine structures, we find that every event is itself already determined and made possible by prior structures."[38] No matter how far back we go, even if we try to imagine an originary event that might have given rise to a grounding structure, we discover that we are at a loss to know where to begin. For we must always assume prior organization, prior differentiation. What we ordinarily take to be present is always already a systematic product of differences.[39] Thus we are, as Derrida notes, constantly forced to shift back and forth between the perspectives of event and structure, which leads not to a synthesis but to *aporia* or undecidability.[40]

As a general strategy, deconstruction seeks to expose the inherent contradictions in a text which must be repressed if the text is to be given a univocal interpretation. The deconstructionist points to the fundamental tendency in all metaphysical discourse to repress its *other*. As Christopher Norris explains: "Derrida seeks to disabuse us of the delusions engendered by naive ontologies of language. Deconstruction sets out to demonstrate that meaning can never coincide with its object in a moment of pure, unimpeded union; that language always intervenes to deflect, defer, or differentially complicate the relation between manifest sense and expressive intent."[41] This has profound implications not only for the act of interpretation, but also for the act of self-interpretation. For if meaning is unmasterable, then the author's authority over a text is undermined in a radical way. This form of criticism not only denies interpretive privilege to authors, it denies that there can be any fundamental unity in a text on the grounds that every text already contains the seeds of its own deconstruction.

In a recent essay entitled "Points of View for His Work as an Author,"[42] Louis Mackey challenges the notion that there is any fundamental unity in Kierkegaard's authorship. Despite Kierkegaard's own claim that the strictly religious works provide the point of view from which the others are to be understood, Mackey argues that "the simple contradiction between the aesthetic and the religious writings does not by itself establish an ordering of the texts and an allocation of priorities" (185). The supposed "organic unity" of the authorship is an illusion created by the repression of difference within the text itself. The problem is not so much that Kierkegaard presumes the authenticity of his account, but that he "presupposes the *possibility* of an authenticity—a singleness of purpose and a coincidence of purpose and performance—against which his experience as the master of a whole troop of pseudonyms . . . should have cautioned him" (187).

Mackey agrees with Fenger, who claims that Kierkegaard's privileging word "adds just another to the religious works and therefore cannot legitimately ask to be taken as the transcendent perspective that unifies the canon" (186). The difference between their views is that, whereas Fenger points to the "false unity" in Kierkegaard's writings, Mackey contends that there is no unity at all. In the authorship, the distinction between aesthetic and religious modes of discourse is strictly undecidable. Mackey reasons as follows:

> There is perhaps never good reason (even in the "normal" case) to identify the "writer" with the "actual" person whose name he signs, though it is natural to do so. But in the [case of Kierkegaard] the course of nature is blocked by the flagrant interposition of artifice. . . . The proliferation of artifice makes the distinction undecidable and the identity of the natural indeterminable. When a man fabricates as many masks to hide behind as Kierkegaard does, one cannot trust his (purportedly) direct asseverations. And when he signs his own name, it no longer has the effects of the signature. (188)

Thus Kierkegaard's rhetoric at once asserts and undermines its own performance. His authorship offers us a striking example of how texts are always already in the process of deconstructing themselves.

A similar type of reading is offered by Christopher Norris, who compares the autobiographical narrative of Kierkegaard's *Point of View* to Rousseau's *Confessions*, discerning in the former the same 'subversive' logic that Paul de Man finds in the latter. Norris summarizes his view in the following passage:

> The duplicity of language is always in excess of the elaborate strategies which Kierkegaard adopts to explain and justify his authorial conduct. Thus *The Point of View*, by its complex "dialectical" reordering of memories and motives, creates a text

which partakes as much of fiction as of spiritual self-revelation. De Man describes this alienating logic of narrative contrivance as it affects the writing of Rousseau's *Confessions*. "This threatens the autobiographical subject not as the loss of something that was once present and that it once possessed, but as a radical estrangement between the meaning and the performance of any text." It is especially impossible to decide just how much in *The Point of View* is dictated by a logic of narrative self-vindication basically at odds with Kierkegaard's idea of existential good faith.[43]

However, as Norris also points out, there are other aspects of Kierkegaard's position that make it impossible finally to reconcile him with the deconstructionist project. "It should be obvious," he writes, "that Kierkegaard carries deconstruction only to the point where its strategies supposedly come up against an undeconstructible bedrock of authenticated truth."[44] Underlying the celebrated distinction between objectivity and subjectivity (and the subsequent identification of truth with the latter) is the view that there exists an absolute truth, and that it is possible to be related to this truth in time. The absolute truth cannot be realized through metaphysical speculation, nor through direct communication from one individual to another, but only through the ethical-religious striving of faith.

Accordingly, Kierkegaard does not attempt to communicate directly the truth about human existence, but rather to enable others to discover that truth for themselves by removing the illusion that obscures the real requirements of faith. In *The Point of View*, Kierkegaard explains that "there is a difference between writing on a blank sheet of paper and bringing to light by the application of a caustic fluid a text which is hidden under another text."[45] He complains that the "dishonesty of the age" can be seen in the fact that it attempts to communicate ethical-religious truth directly, as though writing on a blank sheet of paper.[46] But this type of truth can only be appropriated by the existing individual, who recreates it in self-activity. In order to facilitate this activity in his readers, Kierkegaard uses an indirect form of discourse designed to force the reader to turn inward, to rediscover what he refers to as "the original text of the individual human existence-relationship, the old text (*Urskrift*). . . ."[47]

The very idea of revealing the text behind the text is highly problematic for the deconstructionist. What is to guarantee that the removal of one illusion will not merely result in its replacement by another? Nietzsche poses this question in its most acute form by extending the metaphor of textuality to nature and history. Taken in conjunction with the perspectiv-ist thesis that there is only interpretation, Nietzsche's textualism has the far-reaching implication that there can be no text behind the text, no *Ur-*text. He asks, Why not simply regard the world as a fiction? And if it is suggested that fiction implies an originator, an author, why not suppose that this, too, belongs to the fiction?[48] The proper task of the philosopher, he tells us in *Beyond Good and Evil*, is "to become master over the many vain and overly enthusiastic interpretations and connotations that have so far been scrawled and painted over that eternal basic text [*ewigen Grund-text*] of *homo natura* . . . "[49] Nietzsche not only stresses the epistemological point that all knowing is limited by one's perspective, and hence that all interpretations are essentially incomplete; he goes on to claim that there are no rational grounds for believing in the existence of those things phi-losophers have traditionally employed to ground interpretations of self and world (including, preeminently, the concept of a Divine Author). Regarding the text of *homo natura* there can be no complete or final per-spective, since all texts are constantly in the process of being rewritten. For Nietzsche, to "become master over the many vain and overly enthusiastic interpretations" means to have the courage to explore the limitless play of intertextuality, through which one acquires a deeper understanding of the textual labyrinth that is human existence.

This is precisely the point at which Kierkegaard parts company with deconstructive criticism, which denies the existence of a grounding authenticity. He does not deny that language has the power to mislead, or to create illusion. Deception, he tells us, extends just as far as the truth. But there is a trivial sense in which these statements are true. For we all know that words can be uttered with very different intentions. This admission does not, however, commit Kierkegaard to the undecidability of meaning. Indeed, as a religious writer he regards himself as an instrument of divine Providence whose mission is to make others aware. Providence grounds Kierkegaard's faith in an end to the duplicities of meaning and motive; it ensures that "a tree shall be known by its fruits."

Anticipating the deconstructionist, Kierkegaard acknowledges that if a person is not circumspect in the use of mystification, he may soon find himself in the comical situation of becoming a mystery to himself. But this, Kierkegaard insists, is attributable to a lack of seriousness, which "prompts him to fall in love with mystification for its own sake," instead of using it for a higher purpose. Hence, he writes, "when a mystification . . . is used in the service of a serious purpose, it will be so used as merely to obviate a misunderstanding . . . whereas all the while the true explanation is at hand and ready to be found by him who honestly seeks it."[50] Thus, as Norris points out, "there is always a decisive moment of advance from 'indirect communication' to truth directly apprehended and thus no longer subject to the ruses and dangers of reflection. To ignore this moment . . . is to prove oneself lacking in the 'serious' powers of mind requisite to a higher understanding."[51] The "unreconstructed aesthete," who prefers to play with possibilities and then leave them all unactualized, reveals just such a lack of seriousness. In Kierkegaard's judgment, this is not merely an intellectual shortcoming, it is a moral failure.

There is a striking parallel here between Kierkegaard's position and recent attempts to respond to the deconstructionist on moral and theological grounds. George Steiner, for example, has argued persuasively that without the assumption of presence "certain dimensions of thought and creativity are no longer attainable. . . . We must read *as if*."[52] In his view, any coherent understanding of what language is and how it functions is underwritten by the assumption of presence (3). Indeed, all meaningful encounters with art, literature, and music must presuppose this presence.

Like Kierkegaard, Steiner is aware that there is no end to the possibility of interpretive disagreement. This is an unavoidable feature of all human communication:

> Our encounter with the freedom of presence in another human being . . . will always entail approximation. . . . The congruence is never complete. It is never uniform with its object. If it was, the act of reception would be wholly equivalent to that of original enunciation. . . . The falling-short is a guarantor of the experienced "otherness". . . . (175)

But we must also recognize that aesthetic understanding, like any authentic act of human understanding, has a profoundly moral dimension. Interpretation involves a commitment, it requires a response which is, as the word itself suggests, *responsible*. A serious reader must be willing to take risks, to be open to the spirit of the text, allowing himself to be touched by the presence of the other (148,177).These remarks not only echo Kierkegaard's concern about the moral aspect of reading, they also fit well with the theological presuppositions that underlie the production of the authorship.

At the very least, it can be said that Kierkegaard stands in a highly ambiguous relation to current theories of reading and textuality. On the one hand, he anticipates many of the claims of deconstructive criticism.

This is especially evident in his renunciation of interpretive authority with respect to his own texts, but also in his relentless criticism of all metaphysical attempts to systematize existence. On the other hand, however, he provides the reader with a viewpoint that renders deconstruction "at best redundant, and at worst a species of mischievous 'aesthetic' distraction."[53] Kierkegaard's appeal to a providential ethics of reading, his faith in the existence of an originary text behind the text, poses a formidable challenge to deconstructionist strategies of textual demystification (105f.).

PRESENCE IN ABSENCE:
A STRATEGY FOR READING KIERKEGAARD

How then are we to read Kierkegaard? To understand the sense in which Kierkegaard is *present* in the authorship, we must first understand the sense in which he is *absent* from it. Here we must say a word about the art of "indirect communication." This art

> consists in making oneself, the communicator, into a nobody, purely objective, and then continually placing the qualitative opposites in a unity. This is what some pseudonymous writers are accustomed to calling the double reflection of the communication. For example, it is indirect communication to place jest and earnestness together in such a way that the composite is a dialectical knot–and then to be a nobody oneself. If anyone wants to have anything to do with this kind of communication, he will have to untie the knot himself. Or, to bring attack and defense into a unity in such a way that no one can directly say whether one is attacking or defending, so that the most zealous supporter of the cause and its most vicious foe can both seem to see in one an ally–and then to be nobody oneself, an absentee, an objective something, a nonperson.[54]

In either case the communicator cancels out, leaving the reader with a dialectical knot that cannot be undone merely by reference to Kierkegaard. The purpose of the indirect communication is to get the reader to see that ethical-religious truth lies in the realm of inwardness and subjectivity, and hence that it must be appropriated by the individual. To the extent that such a communication is successful, the communicator will have been merely an occasion for the reader to make this movement. Kierkegaard's model for the indirect form of communication is the maieutic method of Socrates.[55]

Each pseudonymous text is brought forth from the perspective of its author, and is then opened up to interpretation and appropriation from the perspective of its reader. In this way, Kierkegaard recognizes the efficacy of the incomplete as a stimulus for transforming those who read his works. I have suggested that Kierkegaard remains consistent on this point by reducing his own status to that of a reader, and hence one more perspective. On this point, at any rate, Kierkegaard is in substantial agreement with Nietzsche's view that an author's true task is not merely to impart information, but to be an occasion for the reader's self-activity. The conscientious author will always seek to play a subordinate role in the communication process, to serve merely as a contributing factor in the interpretation of the text. For Kierkegaard, writing emerges as a means of communication, not in the sense of a direct transmission of meaning or truth between individuals or between text and reader, but rather as an incitement to further activity in and through the individual's subjective appropriation of ethical-religious truth.

In keeping with his indirect strategy, Kierkegaard does not himself choose between the aesthetic and ethical-religious perspectives. In the pseudonymous works, the contradiction of viewpoint remains unresolved. The pseudonyms thus achieve a kind of ideality that creates poetic distance between the writing self and the written word. "An author," Kierkegaard says, "certainly must have his private personality as everyone else has, but this must be his . . . [inner sanctum], and just as the entrance to a house is barred by stationing two soldiers with crossed bayonets, so by means of the dialectical cross of qualitative opposites the equality of ideality forms the barrier that prevents all access."[56] It does not follow from this, however, that Kierkegaard did not have a specific agenda, or that the authorship was not guided by the religious purpose claimed for it in *The Point of View*. But how does this idea of religious purpose manifest itself in the authorship?

I want to suggest that what Kierkegaard created, consciously or unconsciously, in the process of writing was an implied version of himself. When we read the authorship as a totality, we discover that each work fits into a larger design, which traces out the various moments of an existential dialectic in pursuit of authentic selfhood. Kierkegaard specifically draws our attention to this design in support of his religious interpretation of the authorship. It is, he believes, a design that suggests one kind of author rather than another, or what Wayne C. Booth has aptly termed an "implied author."

The implied author, as Booth explains, is the organizing principle that gives us a sense from line to line, from book to book, that the author "sees more deeply and judges more profoundly than his presented characters."[57] We infer this author as "an ideal, literary, created version of the real man; he is the sum of his own choices" (75). As a reader of the authorship, Kierkegaard picks out an implied author with whom he identifies himself in the autobiographical writings. Whether or not we accept this interpretation as sincere will depend on whether Kierkegaard has succeeded in establishing the integrity of this author.

Appeal to the concept of an implied author avoids the problem of having to "get it right" in the sense that one latches onto the actual authorial intention behind the work. For the implied author is at once distinct from both the pseudonym and the historical writer. This concept also avoids the problem of what to do with texts without access to authors, as well as the problem of how to judge the sincerity of their authors. Booth and Kierkegaard agree that the literary text is the best evidence we have concerning authorial intention and sincerity. This point is elaborated by Booth in a passage that deserves quoting at length:

> It is only by distinguishing between the author and his implied image that we can avoid pointless and unverifiable talk about such qualities as "sincerity" or "seriousness" in the author. . . . But we have only the work as evidence for the only kind of sincerity that concerns us: Is the implied author in harmony with himself—that is, are his other choices in harmony with his explicit narrative character? If a narrator who by every trustworthy sign is presented to us as a reliable spokesman for the author professes to believe in values which are never realized in the structure as a whole, we can then talk of an insincere work. A great work establishes the "sincerity" of its implied author, regardless of how grossly the man who created that author may belie in his *other* forms of conduct the values embodied in his work. For all we know, the only sincere moments of his life may have been lived as he wrote his novel. (75)

Similarly, if Kierkegaard had professed in *The Point of View* to believe in and promote religious values which were never realized in the authorship, then we could raise the question of insincerity. I contend that the internal structure of the authorship is essentially in harmony with the retrospective account Kierkegaard offers us in his autobiographical writings. The pseudonymous authorship does in fact establish the sincerity of its implied author, regardless of how grossly the historical Kierkegaard may have belied in his other forms of conduct the moral and religious values embodied in it. In the remaining chapters, all references to Kierkegaard should be understood as references to this implied author.

The problem with current deconstructionist readings of Kierkegaard is not that they ascribe to his authorship an indeterminacy of meaning which he would find unacceptable, but rather that they obscure the theoretical assumptions which inform his writing. These include the distinction between literary and nonliterary forms of discourse; the affirmation of the logical and semantic priority of the literary text; the view of the author as reader; and the appeal to an operative or implied author, which is revealed only indirectly in the text.

However, a more important difference between Kierkegaard and deconstructive criticism can be seen in the moral and theological assumptions that shape his view of reading and interpretation. In the light of the nihilistic alternative presented by deconstruction, Kierkegaard urges us to make the interpretive leap of faith and "wager on transcendence."[58] And he does so out of a profound conviction that to break with the "postulate of the sacred," as Steiner calls it, is to forfeit that theological criterion of meaning which underlies the very possibility of authentic selfhood.

Having arrived at a strategy for reading Kierkegaard, we turn now to an examination of the philosophical scope of the authorship.

2

❧

Kierkegaard as Christian Philosopher

It is the main contention of this study that Kierkegaard presents a coherent and philosophically interesting view of the nature of Christian revelation, and of the religious form of life that is defined by reference to that central concept. In this chapter I shall attempt to explain the sense in which Kierkegaard may be regarded as a philosopher in the service of Christianity.

I suggested in the preceding chapter that the philosophical scope of Kierkegaard's writing can be defined within the context of the purpose he envisioned for himself as a Christian author. In *The Point of View*, Kierkegaard characterizes that purpose in the following terms:

> The contents of this little book affirm, then, what I truly am as an author, that I am and was a religious author, that the whole of my work as an author is related to Christianity, to the problem of becoming a Christian, with a direct or indirect polemic against the monstrous illusion we call Christendom, or against the illusion that in such a land as ours all are Christians of a sort.[1]

The "monstrous illusion" refers to the fact that in Kierkegaard's day all are Christians as a matter of course, despite the fact that the majority no longer live Christian lives. The very medium for being Christian has been "shifted from existence and the ethical to the intellectual, the metaphysical . . . and thus being a Christian has been abolished."[2] This is not to say that Christianity has been abolished. As Kierkegaard explains: "Christianity is still present and in its truth, but as a *teaching*, as *doctrine*. What has been abolished and forgotten, however (and this can be said without exaggeration), is *existing as a Christian*, what it means to be a Christian."[3] Christianity has been transformed from an ethical concern which affects the existence of every individual to a subject for speculative, historical, and aesthetic inquiry.

According to Kierkegaard, this illusion is engendered by a "volatilization" of the language of Christian discourse:

> If it is factual that the language of Christian concepts has become in a volatilized sense the conversational language of the whole of Europe, it follows quite simply that the holiest and most decisive definitions are used again and again without being united with the decisive thought. One hears indeed often enough Christian predicates used by Christian priests where the names of God and of Christ constantly appear and passages of Scripture, etc., in discourses which nevertheless as a whole contain pagan views of life without either the priest or the hearers being aware of it.[4]

Kierkegaard's complaint is that Christianity no longer poses a challenge to the comforts of a self-centered, worldly existence. Though his contemporaries continue to talk about "sin" and "salvation," they employ these concepts without a genuine consciousness of sin, or of the need for salvation. Though they regard themselves as Christians, they no longer possess true Christian understanding, and no longer live their lives within the categories of Christian faith.

The source of this illusion is traced to a gradual assimilation of Christian discourse into the prevailing categories of Hegelian idealism. Due to the careless mixing of metaphysical and religious categories, the age has lost sight of the decisive content of Christianity. In order to combat the illusion of Christendom, Kierkegaard sets out to do two things. First, he attempts to expose the ethical and religious inadequacies of all idealist attempts to explain what it means to be a Christian. He then proceeds to clarify Christian concepts in their own right, so as to bring out their decisive significance for the religious life. This twofold task is begun by the pseudonym Johannes Climacus, who takes aim at Hegel's philosophical system.

PHILOSOPHICAL OBJECTIONS TO HEGEL

Perhaps the most concise definition of what a system is can be found in the *Critique of Pure Reason*, where Kant explains: "By a system I understand the unity of the manifold modes of knowledge under one idea. This idea is the concept provided by reason—of the form of a whole—in so far as the concept determines *a priori* not only the scope of its manifold content, but also the positions which the parts occupy relatively to one another."[5] The result, which is not a mere aggregate knowledge but an organic unity, qualifies this knowledge as science (*Wissenschaft*). According to Hegel, philosophy must be a systematic science, because the absolute idea itself constitutes a system, and it is the task of philosophy to mirror the structure of that system.[6]

At the heart of Hegel's philosophy is the view that thought is the self-mediation of being, that the reality of being inheres in the concept and can be grasped only in rational thought. In short, the real is the rational. It is not surprising, then, that in his *Lectures on the Philosophy of Religion*, which were written during the last decade of his life, Hegel acknowledged the deep affinity between his system and the "ontological argument."[7] The details of this argument had already been worked out in the *Logic*. As Quentin Lauer explains:

> The thinking with which the *Logic* is concerned from beginning to end is infinite activity. But, infinite activity is the activity of an infinite subject, whose object, too, is infinite. Thought is truly thought only if it is infinite being. Thus, the *Logic* is the detailed working out of the "ontological argument," the proof of God from the infinity of thought.[8]

This rational form of proof is to be distinguished from what Hegel calls a proof of the understanding, which is limited to the content of formal concepts, and from which no conclusion can be drawn concerning the nature of reality. To the extent that the concept of God is seen as a formal, abstract object for thought, Hegel agrees with Kant (and Kierkegaard) that nothing follows about God's nature or existence. But to *think* God, which is the task of philosophy, is to think God's thinking in me, it is God's revelation of the divine nature in rational thought. Thus, for Hegel, religion is completed in philosophy: "If human knowing is to be truly knowing it must in some sense be divine. This it is in religion, but religion itself can ultimately know what it is knowing only in and through philosophy, which is to say that in religion man *believes* in God, but only in philosophy can he *know* what God (in whom he believes) is" (275). It is in this sense that Hegel can affirm the superiority of philosophical understanding, while maintaining that the content of philosophy and religion are essentially one and the same. The God which religion thinks only figuratively is the same God which philosophy grasps conceptually.

But even though God reveals the divine nature to the individual in thought, it must be remembered that the individual *qua* individual is limited, and hence that the manner in which the divine spirit is revealed in the individual is limited as well (268). Lauer reminds us that for Hegel,

> the individual is significant only as integrated in the community, never as isolated (or abstracted) from it. For Hegel, to be a Christian is to be in the Christian community; it is not to make some sort of individual response to a God who seems scarcely distinguishable from the response, it is to be in and of the community which responds. . . . It is the individual who as finite is bearer of the infinite, but this he does not by a "leap" beyond his finitude. Rather, it is through the mediation of the community in which individuality is realized that his very finitude is a passage to the infinite—or else it is an abstraction. (290–291)

This latter point is crucial, for it not only underscores the fact that Hegel sees the individual as subordinate to the community, but more importantly, it reveals that the study of logic abstracts from the particular forms that truth takes in finite minds. The ascent to the absolute is the dialectical progress toward God's "self-knowing truth," which is realized through the mediation of the human community.[9]

The general focus of Kierkegaard's criticism is the assumption that the categories of logic are descriptive of reality. Hegel attempts to combine thought and being into a system of pure thought. But Kierkegaard argues that the subject doing this pure thinking could only be a divine being, one that is capable of surveying the world *sub specie aeterni*, not a human being firmly located within history. As Hermann Diem points out, Hegel's grand dialectic of being can only be set in motion and kept in motion by virtue of the illusion that existence can be adequately described in the medium of abstraction. Hegel is guilty of leaving the existence of the thinker totally out of account. The reality that he overlooks, for which he substitutes the fantastic pseudoreality of pure thought, is the reality of the individual thinker who exists and must contemplate his own existence in order to live in it.[10]

According to Hegel's dialectic, the movement of becoming results from the inherent instability of the concept of pure being, with which the dialectic begins. As a contentless abstraction, the concept of pure being is entirely empty; it is nothing. The result is that being passes into, and out of, its opposite, and this continual oscillation gives rise to the movement of becoming. But Kierkegaard challenges the claim that actual movement can arise from the interaction of static concepts, arguing that Hegel blurs the distinction between a ground (reason) and a cause. According to Wolff's original definition, a ground "is that by which one can understand why something is, and the cause is a thing that contains in itself the ground of another thing."[11] In accordance with the traditional view, Kierkegaard shows that logical movement, which is a movement from premises to conclusions, is characterized by necessity; it is a movement from one possibility to another that is mediated entirely within the realm of pure thought. But this is to be distinguished from *kinesis*, which expresses the actual transition from possibility to actuality.[12] The transition of coming into existence occurs not by necessity, but as the result of a freely acting cause.[13] This point is central to the argument of the *Fragments*, where it is shown that transitions of an ethical and religious kind are examples of movement in the latter sense. In this form of movement, the individual must choose to actualize one possibility rather than another, to translate thought into action. In Christianity, where the emphasis is on personal conversion, repentance, and rebirth, the individual must make an existential decision, which cannot be mediated in pure thought. Here, the emphasis rests squarely on *becoming* a Christian.

The foregoing argument is developed more fully in the *Postscript*, where special reference is made to the work of Trendelenburg, a German Aristotelian philosopher, whose critical exposition of Hegel's *Logic* was formative in Kierkegaard's thinking during this period.[14] A prominent objection is directed to Hegel's claim that philosophy has an absolute and presuppositionless beginning. Kierkegaard argues that such a beginning cannot be made immediately, for if the system is "presumed to come after existence, . . . then the System is of course *ex post facto*, and so does not begin immediately with the immediacy with which existence began."[15] Nor can an immediate beginning be made with the help of reflection, since reflection is infinite and cannot bring itself to a halt.[16] Only a resolution of the will in the form of a leap can break the endless chain of reflective thought. But then the beginning is *eo ipso* not presuppositionless, since it has been brought about by a transition from one genus to another.[17] And finally, it will not do to define the "immediate" as the result of a process of abstraction, whereby one finally arrives at the indeterminate content of pure being, since this act of abstraction must be infinite as well. Kierkegaard explains that "if it is at all possible for a human being to abstract from everything in his thinking, it is at any rate impossible for him to do more, since if this act does not transcend human power, it absolutely exhausts it."[18]

As an organic unity, the system constitutes a single whole, the individual moments of which stand in a mutually supporting relationship. But how is an existing individual, limited by the temporal conditions of existence, to survey this whole simultaneously? Whereas existence is defined by the temporal, whose moments are discrete and successive, "systematic thought consists of the finality which brings them together."[19] Only by abstracting from existence and the temporal can one arrive at an eternal vantage point from which to survey all the moments of time. Existence may therefore be a system for God, but it cannot be so for a finite human being. The problem with Hegel's philosophy is not that it is mistaken in assuming that existence can be surveyed systematically, but that it has a "comical presupposition, occasioned by its having forgotten . . . what it means to be a human being."[20]

To the foregoing objection it might be replied that philosophy, as a science, is a corporate activity. As Michael Inwood points out, a system is not "put together" by a philosopher, rather "he reveals interconnections intrinsic to it, and puts together only what has been separated by previous thinkers," so that when the particular sciences "have purified their concepts sufficiently, they will 'mirror the concept,' and fall into place as parts of a single science."[21] But Kierkegaard anticipates this move. For what, he asks, are the categories which "mediate between the individual and world-process, and who is it again who strings them all together on the systematic thread? Is he a human being or is he speculative philosophy in the abstract?"[22] Kierkegaard's question draws our attention once again to the curious relationship between the individual and the system.

A more serious objection is that the Hegelian speculative view is inconsistent with the Christian understanding of human nature and existence. Whereas Hegel sees the individual as a dialectical mediation of soul, consciousness, and spirit, Kierkegaard views the individual as a "synthesis" of irreconcilable opposites. In *Sickness Unto Death*, this synthesis is described as a unity of freedom and necessity, of time and eternity, of finitude and infinity, in the medium of spirit.[23] But to be a fully actualized self means more than merely being such a synthesis. Spirit manifests itself only when the synthesis is constituted as a relationship that relates itself to itself.[24] That is, to be a fully integrated self requires that one consciously affirm one's selfhood. As James Collins explains, the actualization of spirit involves a free and personal commitment of the will, which is accomplished in acts of moral resolution.[25] The self is essentially an expression of freedom.[26] By actualizing one possibility rather than another, by realizing the ideality of thought in concrete action, the individual defines his personality. Through such acts of moral resolution, the individual is said to "choose himself."[27] The most decisive form of this movement is the act of repentance, which is possible only in the encounter with the God-man of the incarnation.

Whereas Kierkegaard defines actuality as a synthesis of possibility and necessity which is constituted in freedom, Hegel maintains that the possible is the actual, and that freedom must be subsumed under the category of necessity. Kierkegaard contends that by introducing necessity into the historical process, "the categories of possibility, of actuality, and of necessity have all been compromised."[28] By mediating existence in the timeless categories of logical thought, Hegel undermines the radical freedom of the individual, and hence the possibility of authentic selfhood. This point is elaborated by John D. Caputo, who notes that

> Hegelian time lacks what is truly proper to time: contingency, freedom, exposure to the future. It pays public homage to history and temporality while in private it subverts them, subordinating them to a rational teleology which monitors and controls their movements. Hegelian time is reworked by metaphysics, made over into its image and likeness, and in which the groundlessness of radical freedom, which belongs to the essence of time and *kinesis*, is revoked.[29]

Whereas philosophical idealism, from Plato to Hegel, attempts to cope with the flux of existence by retreating to the sphere of immanence, Kierkegaard shows that the real task is *repetition*, which is described as "the power of the individual to forge his personality out of the chaos of events, in the midst of the flux, the power to create an identity in the face of the incessant 'dispersal' of the self, of the dissipating effects of the flux."[30] The secret desire of the system is to arrest the flux, to annul the movement that makes existence difficult. It does this precisely by translating existence into the abstract medium of thought.[31] But thought deals only with that which is final and complete, and hence it is essentially backward-looking.[32] Though life can be understood retrospectively, Kierkegaard's criticism reminds us that it must be lived forward.[33] The existing individual, as a temporal being, must confront his future in the condition of freedom, and determine what that future will be like through his own self-activity.

THE NATURE OF KIERKEGAARD'S CRITIQUE

We must grant right away that Kierkegaard probably did not have a very extensive first-hand knowledge of Hegel's philosophy. Niels Thulstrup and others have shown that Kierkegaard's views about Hegel were formed largely on the basis of his reading of secondary sources.[34] Apart from the aforementioned interest in Trendelenburg, there is evidence that Kierkegaard was influenced by the work of the Danish Hegelians J. L. Heiberg, H. L. Martensen, A. P. Adler, and especially the anti-Hegelian F. C. Sibbern.[35] In an essay published in the *Maanedsskrift for Litteratur* (1838), Sibbern advanced a series of arguments against Hegel, many of which would reappear in Kierkegaard's own critique.[36] A prominent criticism in that piece concerned Hegel's alleged denial of the principle of contradiction. In good logical fashion, Sibbern pointed out that Hegel could not deny the principle of contradiction without implicitly assuming its validity. As Kierkegaard would later formulate the point: The proposition that the principle of contradiction is cancelled must already presuppose the principle of contradiction, for otherwise the proposition that it is not cancelled is equally true.[37]

According to Mark C. Taylor, Kierkegaard's view of contradiction underlies the assumption that we must choose between "a monism in which otherness and difference are epiphenomenal and a dualism in which otherness and difference are abiding features of experience which finally can be overcome, if at all, only eschatologically."[38] Having reduced the possibilities to these two, Kierkegaard attributes the former position to Hegel. Taylor contends, however, that such a characterization fails to appreciate the fact that Hegel "walks the fine line between the extremes of undifferentiated monism and abstract dualism or pluralism."[39] If Taylor is correct, where does this leave Kierkegaard's criticism?

It is true that Kierkegaard posits the existence of radical and irreducible difference in the world. It is also true that he discerns in Hegel the subordination of the principle of contradiction to the principle of identity, quoting Hegel's own description of philosophy as a discipline which "pursues studies toward unity."[40] But the purpose of his objection is not to engage Hegel in a metaphysical debate. Rather, his major point seems to be that the speculative understanding of contradiction posits a distinction without a difference. For the kind of contradictions we encounter in existence are dissolved in speculative thought: "Like the giant who wrestled with Hercules, and who lost strength as soon as he was lifted from the ground, the either-or of contradiction is *ipso facto* nullified when it is lifted out of the sphere of the existential and introduced into the eternity of abstract thought."[41] From the point of view of pure thought, pure possibility, there is no absolute either-or.[42] Abstract thought has the characteristic that it "ignores everything except the thought."[43] In this way, speculative logic merely creates the illusion that existential contradictions can be mediated, an illusion that is made possible by the ambiguity of the word *aufheben,* which Hegel frequently uses to describe the mediation of opposites.[44]

The problem is further compounded when this speculative scheme is then transposed back onto existence. For the idea of contradiction is so essential to a proper understanding of existence that one cannot mediate the former without thereby falsifying the true nature of the latter.[45] This point is elaborated in *Two Ages*:

> The existential expression of nullifying the principle of contra-diction is to be in contradiction to oneself. The creative omnip-otence implicit in the passion of absolute disjunction that leads the individual resolutely to make up his mind is transformed into the extensity of prudence and reflection—that is, by know-ing and being everything possible to be in contradiction to oneself, that is, to be nothing at all. The principle of contradic-tion strengthens the individual in faithfulness to himself.[46]

Kierkegaard's argument is aimed at showing that any attempt to unite the categories of thought and being constitutes a distortion of the true existen-tial situation, which constantly forces the individual to choose between unmediated alternatives. Whether Hegel is interpreted as putting forward an undifferentiated monism or, as John Findlay suggests, a "self-pluraliz-ing monism and a self-unifying pluralism,"[47] Kierkegaard's criticism still applies.

We must be careful, however, not to place too much emphasis on Kierkegaard's competence as an interpreter of Hegel. For as James Collins wisely cautions, Kierkegaard did not concern himself very deeply with the technicalities of Hegel's philosophical system. Rather, he studied Hegel "as one studies the *fons et origio* of a broad intellectual and social move-ment."[48] Kierkegaard is much more interested in Hegelianism as an atti-tude, and its implications for our understanding of the ethical and religious dimensions of human experience. His tactic is neither to fight Hegel on his own speculative-idealist terms, which would be futile, nor to beg the ques-tion against him on definitional grounds.[49] The tactic is rather to call attention to the conceptual differences that make it impossible finally to reconcile Christianity and speculative philosophy.

Commenting on the nature of Kierkegaard's philosophical project, Paul Holmer writes:

> An attack on another's philosophy is not in itself unusual. But it is the mode of Kierkegaard's attack which marks him as a philosopher and thinker of first rank. He does not quarrel with particular factual claims within a philosopher's writings nor does he do as rival metaphysicians frequently have done, namely, show that all of the facts can be accounted for by another metaphysical hypothesis. . . . The sallies addressed to the metaphysicians are directed to the logic of their discourse as well as the ethical and religious inadequacies inherent in taking such extravagant claims seriously.[50]

This is most clearly evident in his attack on Hegelian moral philosophy. Whereas Hegel understands the ethical in universal terms, Kierkegaard contends that ethical questions make sense only at the individual level, in so far as they are grounded in the concrete reality of the individual existence.[51] The fundamental confusion of speculative philosophy is that it mistakes "the abstract consideration of a standpoint with existence, so that when a man has knowledge of this or that standpoint he supposes himself to exist in it. . . . From the abstract point of view there is no decisive conflict between the standpoints, because abstraction precisely removes that in which the decision inheres: *the existing subject.*"[52] But experience teaches us that choices must be made.[53] One cannot both pursue the absolute *telos* of the religious life and subscribe to the values of a self-centered, worldly existence: "For this *both-and* means that the absolute *telos* is on the same plane with all the rest. But the absolute *telos* has the remarkable characteristic that it demands acknowledgment as the absolute *telos* every moment."[54] Speculative philosophy simply does not provide a framework within which an existing individual can develop a coherent and meaningful account of his own existence.

Kierkegaard does not deny that it is possible to view humanity as a whole in terms of its historical development, or in terms of what is essential to the race. After all, from a Christian point of view, the doctrine of original sin assumes that "the whole race participates in the individual and the individual in the whole race."[55] However, Kierkegaard is very careful to qualify this point. For sin, no matter how common it is, does not gather human beings into collective association. Rather, it splits them up into "single individuals and holds each individual fast as a sinner, a splitting up that in another sense is both harmonized with and teleologically oriented to the perfection of existence."[56] Although we are all implicated in Adam's guilt, we must acknowledge our sin and seek forgiveness as individuals before God.

It is precisely with regard to the concept of sin that Kierkegaard makes his strongest case against the modern speculative interpretation of Christianity. That Christianity is essentially defined with respect to the concept of sin, and that it therefore addresses itself to the individual, is affirmed throughout Kierkegaard's writings on the subject. In *Sickness Unto Death*, for example, it is explained that sin

> is the category of individuality. Sin cannot be thought speculatively at all. The individual human being lies beneath the concept; and an individual human being cannot be thought, but only the concept 'man'–That is why speculation promptly embarks upon the teaching about the *predominance* of the generation over the individual.[57]

Christianity begins with the teaching about sin, and addresses itself exclusively to the single individual.[58] As soon as we abstract from the category of the individual, Christianity is abolished. For this abstraction creates the illusion that the individual can be related to God through the race, rather than through an individual act of repentance and the ethical-religious striving of faith. If this were possible, then the God-man would be "a phantom instead of an actual prototype."[59]

Kierkegaard reminds us that questions about the ultimate meaning and destiny of human existence are occasions for a certain type of self-examination. They are questions about how an individual ought to shape his existence, and thus provide an occasion for ethical and religious decisions. Christianity frames this decision in terms of the category of sin. But by viewing Christianity without reference to the existence of the individual, and hence without reference to the importance of making ethical and religious decisions–that is, by attempting to explain Christianity as a necessary development in the historical process in which the absolute idea realizes itself–Hegel removes what is essential to the possibility of being Christian, and thereby creates the illusion that faith can be reduced to an intellectual exercise, a form of rational comprehension. To the extent that Christian discourse has become volatilized by a mixing of metaphysical and religious categories, the necessity of *existing as a Christian* has been removed.

PHILOSOPHY IN THE SERVICE OF CHRISTIANITY

In order to reintroduce Christianity into Christendom, a specific strategy is adopted: To confront the individual with "the most decisive definitions of the religious," in order that he might "come to his senses and realize what is implied in calling himself Christian."[60] As Kierkegaard remarks elsewhere, it is his aim to help the reader to attain "a clarity about certain dogmatic concepts and an ability to use them which otherwise is not easily to be had."[61] In short, the strategy involves the clarification of fundamental religious concepts, the concepts which play a decisive role in defining the Christian form of life. Christianity is admittedly a *doctrinal* religion, but faith, according to Kierkegaard, is decidedly an *existential* matter.[62] The decision to become Christian requires the adoption of a principle of practice, the resolve to live one's life in accordance with a religious ideal.

The philosophical scope of Kierkegaard's task, then, is to recover the original and distinctive meanings of Christian concepts, so that their significance for determining the Christian form of life can be made apparent. To this end, Kierkegaard proposes to reintroduce what he calls the ideal picture of being a Christian, to show that Jesus Christ (the "absolute paradox") is the prototype, the object of Christian faith.[63] The task of recovering the distinctive concepts of Christian discourse involves showing how they bear on the way a person lives, contrasting the Christian form of life and discourse with other forms of life and discourse. In this way it can be shown, for example, that a person has no right to continue to speak of himself as a Christian, to continue the volatilized use of Christian terms, so long as he continues to live without regard for the concerns, dispositions, feelings, convictions, and obligations essential to Christian faith. Kierkegaard tries to encourage honesty in his readers (not only to others, but primarily to themselves) about the way they stand in relation to the requirements involved in becoming a Christian, an honesty which reveals itself not only in what one says, but more importantly in how what one says is reflected in one's mode of existence.[64]

In his two books, Johannes Climacus sets out to analyze and clarify the concept most central to Christianity: revelation. On the basis of his analysis, he shows that there are logical reasons why we cannot assess the truth of what is actually given in revelation. The content of revelation transcends human reason and, as such, presents the individual with an absolute paradox. In revelation the individual confronts the unknowable God. Kierkegaard concludes from this that it is inappropriate to approach the decision to become Christian on objective or theoretical grounds. Until the decision to accept Christianity is viewed from the standpoint of subjectivity (the practical-ethical standpoint), where the paradoxical implications of Christian faith are emphasized, one cannot be said to accept Christianity. At best, one can be said to have accepted a doctrine. But Christianity is more than mere doctrine; it is a form of life, a manner of existing and of conceiving of one's existence. The deliberation about whether to become a Christian involves a process of ethical self-reflection that issues in a decision about the sort of person one wants to be or become; a decision to live one's life in accord with the Christian ideal. The absolute paradox forces the realization that one must renounce the false security of a faith bolstered by objective demonstrations and proofs. Faith is a profoundly practical-ethical matter which involves not only the adoption of a principle of practice, but also the resolve to remain in that practice, the practice of faith.

Through this procedure of conceptual clarification, Kierkegaard sheds light on the nature of the relationship between philosophy and Christianity, reason and revelation. He envisions two roles for reason within Christianity. First, although reason cannot judge the actual content of revelation, it can serve in a "negative" capacity, in the sense that by a dialectical process of inquiry it can show what cannot count as a proper object for faith. And second, reason plays a crucial role in determining the limits of meaningful discourse about revelation, in determining what counts as a valid move in the language game about revelation. This is shown by Kierkegaard in *On Authority and Revelation*.

Kierkegaard began writing *On Authority and Revelation* shortly after the publication of the *Concluding Unscientific Postscript.* In the second preface to the book, Kierkegaard characterizes his project in the following terms:

> The whole book is essentially an ethical investigation of the concept of revelation; about what it means to be called by a revelation; about how he who has had a revelation is related to the race, the universal, and we others to him; about the confusion from which the concept of revelation suffers in our confused age. Or, what comes to the same thing, the whole book is an investigation of the concept of authority, about the confu-

sion involved in the fact that the concept of authority has been entirely forgotten in our confused age.[65]

The work focuses on the case of Adler, a Danish pastor who, in 1843, became the center of theological controversy by claiming that a new doctrine had been revealed to him by Jesus Christ. To Kierkegaard's mind, Adler's case is instructive because it clearly reflects the fundamental religious confusion afflicting his age as a whole, a confusion which Kierkegaard attributes to an "imperfect education" in Christian concepts.[66]

The trouble with Adler is that he has become too deeply imbued with the volatilized language of speculative philosophy to be able to speak about Christian revelation with sufficient clarity and circumspection. Kierkegaard writes: "If Mag. A. is regarded as an awakened man in the sense of the Christian religion, his misfortune is just this, that he is not sufficiently and thoroughly acquainted with the language of Christian concepts, that he does not have them under his control."[67] Adler's problem is further compounded by the fact that, as one who is empowered with the authority of an ordained minister, he has failed in his responsibility to be properly educated in dogmatic Christian concepts. He is deficient in knowledge that is essential to the possibility of carrying out the Christian mission to preach and clarify the word of God.

However, Kierkegaard wants to call our attention to the fact that Adler's confusion is indicative of a deeper and more serious problem. For his failure to grasp the concept of religious authority not only points to the fact that he is unprepared to execute the duties of his office and in a real sense poses a threat to the religious community as a disseminator of false attitudes and beliefs about Christianity; it implies also that Adler has failed to grasp the meaning of divine authority and the unqualified obedience that faith requires. In the religious confusion of the age, the concept of authority has been forgotten, and with it the very qualifications for being called by a revelation.[68]

The conceptual confusion exhibited in Adler's claim to a personal revelation is thus viewed by Kierkegaard as a particular instance of a general problem. The problem is that people continue to speak about themselves as Christians, and to characterize their lives in terms of Christian concepts, despite the deep contradiction between their manner of speaking and living and the requirements of Christianity. *On Authority and Revelation* expresses Kierkegaard's belief that the age in which he lived needed to be reeducated in dogmatic Christian concepts and reawakened to the ethical implications of their use.

As Stanley Cavell correctly observes, the originating concern of *On Authority and Revelation* is reflected in the question of how far a person in the present age may be justified in asserting that he has had a revelation.[69] Kierkegaard is clearly concerned about the question of justification. However, he is not concerned about justification in the sense of having adequate grounds for believing that revelation (or some particular revelational experience) is objectively true. The question of "being justified in asserting" is not a matter of determining how probable it is, given certain historical conditions and an individual's psychological makeup, that he either had or will have a revelation. Nor is it a matter of determining whether an individual is religiously prepared to receive a revelation. Religiously speaking, revelation is always improbable; no preparation is possible. As Kierkegaard amply demonstrates, revelation is not an object of discovery; it is not a matter of scientific or mathematical knowledge, nor even a matter of intuition or mystical insight. It is something which comes from beyond. Revelation is neither assessable within human categories of understanding nor predictable through human imagination. It is God's free self-disclosure, the unveiling of an eternal, transcendent truth which otherwise remains hidden from us. In Kierkegaard's view, the question of "being justified in asserting" takes on a different meaning. No matter what happens in an individual's life, no matter what one's religious preparation might be, the question is whether one is *conceptually* prepared to call something a revelation, to assert that something may count as a genuine instance of revelation.

Though the critique of Hegel's philosophy is sometimes understood to mean the total expulsion of philosophical speculation from the religious life, this is not the case. The main point is that "philosophy and Christianity can never be united."[70] Speculative philosophy deals in the sphere of abstract thought. In this sphere, where essence and existence are one, there is no difference between the concept of a thing and its reality. This is characteristic of thought in general, which Kierkegaard sees as "indifferent to existence in the sense of actuality."[71] Thought can only deal with existence by negating it, or by translating it into something conceptual.[72]

However, Kierkegaard does admit a valid role for speculation in the religious life:

> Speculation can present the problems, can recognize that every individual problem is a problem for faith, is compounded and characterized in such a way that it is a problem for faith—and then can submit: Will you believe or not? Fur-

thermore, speculation can supervise and check faith–that is, what is believed in a given moment or is the content of faith– in order to see that there is no rattle-brained mixing with faith of categories which are not objects of faith but, for example, of speculation. . . . Speculation is sighted–and yet only to the extent that it says: Here it is; then it is blind.[73]

Although philosophy is not a substitute for faith, it is essential to clarifying the requirements of faith. Kierkegaard acknowledges here something that is rarely appreciated in his writing: a deep awareness of the value of philosophy to religion. Philosophy is essential to the clarification of the concepts and categories of the Christian theological framework. Kierkegaard can therefore agree with Hegel that religion without philosophy is blind. However, philosophy is a double-edged sword: there is the ever-present temptation to remain in the speculative mode.[74] We must always keep the limitations of philosophy plainly in view.

Kierkegaard's philosophy is a Christian philosophy. He is concerned to identify, order, and elucidate the central concepts and judgments of Christian discourse. The Climacus writings and the book on Adler are written with the purpose of regaining clarity with respect to dogmatic Christian concepts, and making it possible once again to educate about Christianity. Kierkegaard defends dogmatic concepts by restoring them to their original meanings, thereby revealing their decisive significance for the religious life. In particular, he attempts to remove the conceptual confusion that deprives people of the religious grounds for making claims about revelation; a task which theology, under the influence of speculative philosophy, is no longer able to do. It is in this sense that Kierkegaard can be said to be a philosopher in the service of Christianity.

However, even conceding the philosophical nature of Kierkegaard's work, some would deny that the view of revelation put forward in his writings constitutes a valuable contribution to our understanding of that concept, let alone our understanding of the relationship between philosophy (reason) and Christianity (revelation). The opposition takes its point of departure in the popular conception of Kierkegaard as an irrationalist. In the following chapter, I shall attempt to show that the charge of irrationalism is based on a misinterpretation of the absolute paradox.

3

◆◆◆

Reason, Faith, and Revelation

There is a distinguished group of Kierkegaard scholars who regard the Climacus writings as philosophical texts and have studied them as such. Their approach to the study of Kierkegaard as a philosopher is characterized by the crucial assumption that the 'paradox' of the absolute paradox is of a logical variety. On this interpretation, to have faith in Christianity is to believe a proposition which is not only uncertain, but logically impossible. The traditional line on the Climacus writings is that they put forward an irrationalist view of faith.[1]

THE CHARGE OF IRRATIONALISM

The main points of the irrationalist interpretation can be summarized as follows. According to Kierkegaard, there are two possible ways to attain eternal truth: either in objective reflection or in subjective reflection. Since the way of objective reflection is shown to fail in this regard, it is concluded that only subjective reflection is adequate to attain eternal truth. But not just any form of subjectivity will do. Only the subjectivity of Christian faith, which results from reflection on the absolute paradox, can bring one to the highest truth. Here, faith is construed as a "subjective certainty over a proposition involving one's eternal telos, which is objectively uncertain."[2]

If one wishes to be related to the highest truth, then one must seek to cultivate faith. Faith is a condition that reflects the tension between one's subjective passion and the objective uncertainty of one's intentional object. The element of risk is central to this view of faith: "For without risk there is not faith, and the greater the risk the greater the faith; the more objective security the less inwardness (for inwardness is precisely subjectivity), and the less objective security the more profound the possible inwardness."[3] The greater the improbability that some proposition p is true, the greater the volitional effort required to accept it. The very improbability of p repels human reason and forces the believer into the extremity of passion. In order to believe that p, where this proposition is maximally improbable, it must be believed against reason. If this account is correct, then according to Kierkegaard faith in Christianity is irrational.

Whereas some degree of probability greater than one-half is ordinarily regarded as a necessary condition for justification, Kierkegaardian faith appears to require just the opposite. As a form of intense passionate commitment to an objectively uncertain or improbable proposition, faith declares itself opposed to probability, for the latter diminishes the element of risk, and hence also the passion required to believe.[4] In this reconstruction of Kierkegaard's position, the insufficiency of proof and evidence is not only desirable and advantageous in matters of faith, but necessary to a viable faith. Indeed, faith and paradox are on this view a mutual fit.[5]

On the irrationalist account, the absolute paradox is thought to be connected to the logical difficulties inherent in the metaphysics of God incarnate. According to the specifications of the doctrine of incarnation, as codified at the Council of Chalcedon in A.D. 451, Jesus is alleged to have possessed attributes as a man which are the logical complements of other attributes he is alleged to have possessed as God. But it is strictly impossible for any individual to have, at one and the same time, both an attribute and its logical complement. Faith in Christianity is thus thought to involve the believer in a logical contradiction. But if this is the case, then the truth of Christianity is not merely objectively uncertain, it is logically impossible. There is no possibility that it could someday turn out to be true.

According to the irrationalist interpretation, then, Kierkegaard claims that it is possible to believe something while at the same time recognizing that it is a contradiction. Indeed, he claims that Christianity must be affirmed as such. But can one believe both that the doctrine of incarnation is true and that it is logically inconsistent? It might be thought that Kierkegaard advocates a strong form of volitionalism, which says that a person can acquire certain beliefs independently of any evidential considerations by consciously willing to do so.[6] But there are compelling philosophical grounds for thinking that the strong volitionalist thesis is incoherent.

The argument against the strong volitionalist thesis is motivated by the standard view that belief is involuntary, something that happens to a person rather than something a person does. According to Hume,[7] the acquisition of a belief that p is not under our voluntary control. But as Richard Swinburne has pointed out, this is not merely a contingent feature of human psychology; it is a matter of logic.[8] For on the standard view of belief, we may be said to believe a proposition p if and only if we believe that the total evidence at our disposal makes p more probable than any alternative. Our beliefs are properly a function of the set of basic propositions we accept and the degree of confidence we have in those propositions.[9] But if it is assumed that our beliefs are under our voluntary control, then the basic propositions we accept and the degree of confidence we have in those propositions will have to be assumed under our voluntary control as well.

However, the trust we have in our beliefs and our degree of confidence in them rests on the further assumption that they are formed by external factors, that is, independently of us and of our believing them. Thus, if one were to acquire the belief that p simply by willing to do so, one would realize that this belief originated from one's will and so was not determined by whether what it reported was the case. One would know that there was no reason for trusting that belief, and so would not really believe.

Perhaps Kierkegaard could concede the logical impossibility of Christian incarnation on logical grounds but, like Tertullian, believe it precisely because it is impossible. On this strategy, the fact that the doctrine violates certain fundamental principles of logic might be considered a true mark of its supernatural origin. But to claim that a proposition manifests a logical contradiction is to acknowledge that all the evidence counts against it. And, according to the definition of belief noted above, if one believes that all the evidence is against a proposition, then one cannot really believe that it is true. There are logical limits to irrationality.

It would seem that the only alternative, as Brand Blanshard has pointed out, is for the believer to put logic aside.[10] Using this approach, Kierkegaard might concede that although the incarnation is unintelligible and even self-contradictory, the faithful will come to see that it is absolutely true through a passionate commitment of feeling and will. What this calls for, in effect, is an exception to the principle of contradiction. However, the principle of contradiction is either universally valid or it is not valid at all. And if it is not valid, then in no case does the affirmation of a proposition exclude the truth of its denial, since no proposition is true rather than untrue. By rejecting this fundamental principle, all assertion becomes meaningless, including the Christian claim concerning the truth of the incarnation. Thus, Kierkegaard is faced with a dilemma: "If the logic he assumes in his philosophy is valid, then the faith which stands at the summit of 'the stages on life's way' is meaningless. If that irrational faith is accepted, the principles on which faith conducts itself are everywhere impugned."[11]

It does no good here to fall back on the notion of truth as subjectivity. We cannot simply claim that religion is a commitment of feeling and will and that Christianity seeks to intensify the passion of the individual, rather than to induce belief or rational comprehension. Christianity is a doctrinal religion, and as such it requires that one accept the truth of the doctrine of incarnation, which purports to be an objective truth.[12] To reduce truth to the purely noncognitive status of a passionate self-commitment would not save Christianity but, as Blanshard points out, it would largely destroy it:

> For it implies that there are no common truths for Christians to accept, no common principles by which their lives may be guided, indeed no common Deity for them to contemplate and worship. The Kierkegaardian subjectivity would dissolve things away into a set of processes in individual minds where there would be as many Christians as there were persons to exercise their inwardness and their passion.[13]

Though it follows from the traditional notion of divinity that there will be some aspects of mystery attending all Christian claims about God, it does not follow that logical inconsistency is not a clear and decisive mark of falsehood in theological discussion. Any defense of Christianity that claims otherwise rests on a basic confusion.

If, as the irrationalist interpretation contends, the absolute paradox is intended to express what is *contra rationem*, then it is difficult to see any useful application that the results of Kierkegaard's inquiry can have for understanding the requirements of faith, except to show that the believer is one who embraces nonsense. But this interpretation appears to be deficient in several ways. To begin with, it is clearly affirmed both in the Climacus writings and throughout the *Journals and Papers* that the Christian does not believe mere nonsense. In the former, it is explained that the believer "not only possesses but uses his understanding . . . to make sure that he believes against the understanding. Nonsense therefore he cannot believe against the understanding, for precisely the understanding will discern that it is nonsense and will prevent him from believing it."[14] In the latter, it is plainly asserted that the paradox of Christianity is so constituted that "reason has no power at all to dissolve it," and hence, cannot reduce it to mere nonsense.[15]

Next, Kierkegaard nowhere calls for the suspension of the principle of contradiction. On the contrary, he affirms that true contradictions can never be united and that the principle of contradiction is always valid:

> This is something that our age has altogether overlooked, in and by its repudiation of the principle of contradiction, failing to perceive what Aristotle nevertheless pointed out, namely that the proposition: the principle of contradiction is annulled, itself rests upon the principle of contradiction, since otherwise the opposite proposition, that it is not annulled, is equally true.[16]

But it hardly follows from this that the paradox of Christianity is a logical contradiction. Such an interpretation simply fails to recognize that the terms *contradiction* and *self-contradiction* have a significantly broader use in Kierkegaard's conceptual vocabulary than the narrowly logical one.[17] But more importantly, it fails to recognize that the word *paradox* is used almost exclusively by Kierkegaard in its etymological sense.[18] Far from denoting a necessary falsehood, Kierkegaard affirms that the Christian paradox is an absurdity that must be true.[19]

Finally, the irrationalist interpretation is at odds with the religious purposes Kierkegaard claims for his authorship. The main purpose, which is revealed in *The Point of View*, is to win people over to Christianity. But Kierkegaard could not reasonably have expected to win converts to the faith by portraying the believer as one who embraces nonsense.

Still, the characterization of Christianity as in some sense paradoxical or absurd is in accord with the larger Christian purpose Kierkegaard claimed for his authorship. For the Climacus writings in particular are intended to expose the religious inadequacies of the speculative outlook, which assumes that "understanding" is higher than faith, or the key to a more profound expression of faith.[20] The terms paradox and absurd are thus introduced as a conceptual means of indicating that God's appearance in the temporal order transcends the possibilities of human knowledge, and that it cannot be grasped at a purely intellectual level.[21] Kierkegaard's strategy is clearly not to demonstrate the impossibility of accepting the truth of Christianity, but the impossibility of appropriating that truth on purely objective or intellectual terms. By showing faith to be an existential as opposed to a speculative enterprise, he attempts to remove the confusion that prevents people from seeing the true requirements of faith; requirements that are far more exacting than their speculative substitutes.

In the following section I shall present textual evidence in support of the thesis that Kierkegaard did not intend the absolute paradox to be understood as a logical contradiction.

THE SUPRARATIONALIST INTERPRETATION

In a series of journal entries from 1850, Kierkegaard comments extensively on the meaning of the terms *absurd* and *paradox*. What is significant about this discussion is that Kierkegaard draws a sharp distinction between the absurd of Christianity and what he calls vulgar absurdities or nonsense. He insists, for example, that "not every absurd is the absurd or paradox."[22] One must in fact take great care to define the Christian absurd with accuracy and conceptual correctness. What distinguishes the Christian absurd from vulgar absurdities or nonsense is precisely that it can be believed–by faith. It is directly affirmed that when the believer has faith, "the absurd is not the absurd . . . for . . . faith transforms it."[23] Even though reason cannot grasp what faith believes, there is something about the nature of faith that determines reason to honor it.[24] These remarks clearly suggest that Kierkegaard did not think it possible to believe a logical contradiction, and that to define faith in this way would result in the ultimate identification of Christianity and nonsense.[25] The Christian absurd is, as J. Heywood Thomas has aptly pointed out, "an absurdity that must be true."[26]

What then is the Christian absurd? Kierkegaard explains: "The absurd is the negative criterion of that which is higher than human understanding and knowledge. The operations of understanding are to note it as such–and then submit it to everyone for his belief."[27] The absurd is neither nonsense nor anything that can be known within the categories of human understanding:

> The *absurd*, the *paradox*, is composed in such a way that reason has no power at all to dissolve it in nonsense and prove that it is nonsense; no, it is a symbol, a riddle, a compounded riddle about which reason must say: I cannot solve it, it cannot be understood, but it does not follow thereby that it is nonsense.[28]

The Christian absurd is "a category, the negative criterion, of the divine or of the relationship to the divine."[29] As such it represents a limit to human reason.[30] Kierkegaard characterizes the absolute paradox as a sign of transcendence; a point at which reason realizes its natural limitations. At this juncture it might be suggested that a logical contradiction represents a limit to reason, and in a sense this is true. But it is a different kind of limit altogether from that which Kierkegaard here describes. A paradox in the sense of a logical contradiction occurs within the sphere of reason; it is a point at which reason collides with itself and is thereby brought to a standstill. But Kierkegaard's paradox occurs outside the sphere of reason, it is a point at which reason collides with something foreign to itself, something other. While human reason has recourse to various techniques for dissolving the force of a logical paradox, there is no such recourse in the case of the absolute paradox. For here reason encounters that which has a purely negative determination, that which cannot be thought. As Kierkegaard writes: "The human dialectic cannot advance further than to the admission that it cannot think this . . . but also to the admission that this does not imply anything more than that it cannot think this."[31]

The main point I wish to make here is the following. When Kierkegaard uses the terms *absurd* and *paradox* to characterize the object of Christian faith, he uses them in an extended sense. Revelation is not absurd or even paradoxical in the strict (logical) sense of these terms, but rather in the sense that it absolutely transcends human standards of knowledge (and morality). Revelation is marked by its complete heterogeneity with respect to the purely human order of things. It is the communication of a truth which is so superior that it reveals our judgments (both epistemic and moral) to be in error. Revelation is not absurd or paradoxical in the sense that it stands against reason, but rather in the sense that it stands above reason. Kierkegaard expressly draws such a distinction:

> What I usually express by saying that Christianity consists of paradox, philosophy in mediation, Leibniz expresses by distinguishing between what is above reason and what is against reason. Faith is above reason. By reason he understands, as he says many places, a linking together of truths (*enchainment*), a conclusion from causes. Faith cannot therefore be *proved, demonstrated, comprehended,* for the link which makes a linking together possible is missing, and what else does this say than that it is a paradox.[32]

This point is well documented in the work of a few scholars, who maintain that the absolute paradox is intended to express what is *supra rationem.*[33] The suprarationalist interpretation has been criticized, however, on the grounds that it is too heavily dependent upon Kierkegaard's later journal entries.[34] The implication is that there seems to be a conflict between Kierkegaard's early view of the absolute paradox (e.g. in the *Fragments*) and what he says about that concept in his later writings. In the next section I shall attempt to show that there is in fact substantial agreement between these two accounts.

REEXAMINING THE ABSOLUTE PARADOX

The view Kierkegaard presents of the absolute paradox in the later writings may be characterized briefly as follows: (i) it is 'paradoxical' in some meaningful sense of the term; (ii) it is 'absolute' in some meaningful sense of the term; (iii) it is not a logical contradiction; and (iv) it is such that it can be believed by faith. What follows is a reading of the third chapter of the *Fragments*, in which I attempt to show that the view of the absolute paradox developed there is consistent with the view characterized above.

In the introduction to the Swenson translation of the *Fragments*, Niels Thulstrup summarizes the main question of the book as follows:

> The question is: how is a human being related to the highest truth, whether one possesses it within himself or does not possess it; or, formulated more precisely, in what comprehensive view is it affirmed that man possesses the highest truth and what consequences does this affirmation have, and within what comprehensive view or, more correctly, in what Kerygma is it affirmed that man does not possess the highest truth and what are the consequences of this? . . . The point of departure is in the Socratic (the Platonic, the Idealistic), and thereupon–in Platonic, Greek linguistic forms–Christianity is construed.[35]

According to the Platonic-Socratic model, the existing individual is already in possession of the highest truth and has the power to recover it through a process of introspection and recollection. Christianity sets itself in opposition to the Platonic-Socratic view in two ways: first, by assuming that the existing individual is not in possession of the highest truth; and second, by assuming that such truth can be attained only through divine grace. This distinction sets the stage for Kierkegaard's first formal discussion of the absolute paradox.

Though the entire discussion in the *Fragments* is carried on under the pretense of a hypothesis, there can be no doubt that it presupposes the

Christian account of divine creation, the fall from grace, and the promise of divine forgiveness and reconciliation. The book is largely an exposition of the Christian concept of revelation. In the person of Christ, God reveals not only the fallenness of human beings but also his divine plan for their salvation. The incarnation is God's supreme act of mercy, through which he bestows on human beings the gift of redeeming grace so that they can be regenerated through faith. The individual encounters in Christ a saving truth, which was hitherto unknown and unknowable. But revelation not only creates the possibility for the individual to acknowledge his sinfulness and need for redemption, it also teaches the individual that he is powerless to redeem himself. Only God can make satisfactory atonement, and this is accomplished in the redemptive sacrifice of Christ.[36] The task of faith is for the individual to believe that he has been saved by this unmerited act of divine love, to be inwardly transformed by this saving truth.

The eternal condition by which the individual is saved is therefore made possible in the Christ-revelation. The problem, however, is that the individual's understanding presents a natural obstacle to salvation. In his unregenerate condition, the individual is ignorant of the fact that he exists in sin, and offended at the revelation that he is powerless to extricate himself from the self-imposed bondage of sin. This problem is compounded by the fact that in revelation the individual encounters the absolute paradox.

Kierkegaard begins his exposition of the concept with an observation on the Socratic 'paradox' of self-knowledge. It is observed that Socrates, who devoted his entire life to the pursuit of self-knowledge, finally arrived at the 'paradoxical' conclusion that he could not decide whether he was "a stranger monster than Typhon, or a creature of a gentler and simpler sort, partaking of something divine."[37] Here Kierkegaard clearly has in mind the etymological meaning of 'paradox.' In the original sense of the word, a proposition is said to be paradoxical if it expresses what is contrary to received opinion. To the ancient Greek mind, which regarded man as the measure of all things, it surely must have seemed paradoxical to assert that man cannot know himself. Following this usage, Kierkegaard characterizes the paradox as "the passion of Reason," the passion which strives to discover that which cannot be thought. It stands as an expression for the refusal of reason to recognize its own limitations. This passion must, however, inevitably bring about the downfall of reason.[38]

Kierkegaard goes on to say that the paradoxical is not something to be taken lightly, since it is the very source of the thinker's passion, and that the thinker without passion is but a "paltry mediocrity." More to the point, it is explained that passion has transforming power, and thus represents the possibility for an entirely new point of departure for existence.[39] In reflecting upon what he thought he knew, Socrates encountered something he did not know, namely, the Unknown. Kierkegaard calls this Unknown "the god," though in keeping with the hypothetical nature of the general inquiry he explains that this is nothing more than a name he assigns it.[40] The Unknown cannot be assimilated by the categories of human understanding, since it is "the absolutely different."[41]

The fact that Socrates experiences the paradoxical passion of reason is evidence that he stands in some kind of relationship to the god, the Unknown. But that he is unable to advance further than to the paradoxical realization that he cannot know the highest truth is itself evidence of the inherent conceptual limitations of the Platonic-Socratic view. The highest expression of the fact that Socrates is related to the god is irony.[42]

Christian revelation represents a radically new point of departure for the human understanding of self and God. Negatively, it is intended to teach human beings that they are devoid of the highest truth, that all human points of view are in principle inadequate and need to be corrected with reference to a transcendent point of view.[43] Positively, it is intended to give human beings the condition necessary to attain the highest truth. Christianity assumes that neither the highest truth nor the means to attain it are found in human beings in their natural condition. Human beings cannot even know that they are devoid of the highest truth prior to the communication of this fact in revelation.

In revelation, God reveals himself in the form of an individual human being who is, by all appearances, quite indistinguishable from other human beings. However, that this individual man is also God is something that transcends the possibilities of human knowledge. As Kierkegaard puts it: "This human being is also the god. How do I know that? Well, I cannot know it, for in that case I would have to know the god and the difference, and I do not know the difference inasmuch as the understanding has made it like unto that from which it differs."[44] To claim that the god is knowable is an incoherent claim: "Defined as the absolutely different, it seems to be at the point of being disclosed, but not so, because the understanding cannot even think the absolutely different."[45]

This surely is a paradoxical state of affairs. For in order to know that we are separated from the god by an absolute unlikeness, we require the help of the god. But how are we supposed to acquire knowledge of the divine from one who appears by all accounts to be an ordinary human being?[46] If there is to be any possibility of a reconciliation between the god and human beings, the latter must become conscious of the fact that the absolute unlikeness which separates them from the god is their sin.[47] They must acknowledge that all their judgments are in error and need to be corrected in the light of divine revelation.

Far from claiming that the absolute paradox is a logical contradiction, Kierkegaard offers us the following characterization:

> Thus the paradox becomes even more terrible, or the same paradox has the duplexity by which it manifests itself as the absolute–negatively, by bringing into prominence the absolute difference of sin and, positively, by wanting to annul this absolute difference in the absolute equality. [48]

On this view, the absolute paradox is 'paradoxical' in the (etymological) sense that the god, who is absolutely unlike human beings, reveals himself in a form which appears by all accounts to be knowable.[49] It is 'absolute' in the sense that the god infinitely transcends human knowledge. His divinity cannot be empirically verified; there is no higher explanation of whether revelation is true or of how it is even possible. Where truth is defined as the standard of itself and of falsehood, revelation will be seen to fall outside the circle of possible human knowledge. Thus, Kierkegaard makes the following unambiguous assertion concerning Christian revelation: "Our hypothetical assumption of that fact and the single individual's relation to the god contains no self-contradiction, and thus thought can become preoccupied with it as with the strangest thing of all."[50]

The absolute paradox manifests itself not only as an invincible limit to human reason, but also, and more important for religious purposes, as an "opposition" to human reason. Here, I follow Dr. Swenson in interpreting the Kierkegaardian use of 'reason' not in an abstract-intellectual sense, "but quite concretely, as the reflective organized common sense of mankind, including as its essential core a sense of life's values. Over against the 'Paradox,' it is therefore the self-assurance and self-assertiveness of man's nature in its totality."[51] Thus, revelation is not absurd or paradoxical in the sense that it violates fundamental principles of logic, but in the sense that it disturbs our common sense view of ourselves and our values.

Revelation deliberately undermines the self-assurance of human reason and frustrates our attempts at self-assertion. It does so for the purpose of enabling us to discover that we are in a condition of error, that we suffer from the noetic effects of sin, and that the standards by which we measure ultimate reality are therefore inadequate and need to be transformed in the light of divine revelation. Gordon D. Kaufman comments on this aspect of the doctrine in the following passage:

> From this point of view revelation can be conceived as that which impinges upon us in such a way as to enable us to see the *inadequacy* of all our standards for measuring ultimate reality, and thus it is that which stimulates us to a constant attempt to transform our standards themselves rather than simply to measure everything we meet in terms of them. Revelation, if it is revelation, judges us and our standards; we are in no position to judge it.[52]

This same point is expressed by Kierkegaard in any places. In the *Fragments*, for example, it is asserted that the Christian paradox is properly the standard of itself and of falsehood (*index et judex sui et falsi*).[53] And again in *On Authority and Revelation*, he writes: "The fact that the eternal once came into existence is not something which has to be tested in time, not something which men are to test, but is the paradox by which men are to be tested."[54] When confronted by revelation, reason is left with only two choices: either to acknowledge the impossibility of assimilating revelation to the categories of human understanding, or to reject it. The former choice opens the way to faith, the latter ends in offense.[55]

What remains to be shown is the manner in which Kierkegaard thinks it is possible to believe in Christianity. I suggest that this may be understood along pragmatist lines. As I read Kierkegaard, the absolute paradox lies in the fact that ordinary human standards of truth and knowledge are inadequate to assess the possibility of revelation. God lies beyond the reach of our cognitive resources. In this way, the paradox clears logical space for faith by showing that theoretical reason is incapable of deciding the issue one way or the other. But where theoretical reason cannot decide the option between belief and unbelief, and where eternal happiness hangs in the balance, the venture to believe may be validated on practical grounds. In the following section I shall attempt to characterize the main features of Kierkegaard's pragmatism.

PRAGMATIC REASONS FOR BELIEF

There are doubtless many who will be surprised at the suggestion that there is a pragmatist element in Kierkegaard's thought. One might anticipate several possible objections. It might be objected, first of all, that we do not find in Kierkegaard the straightforward wager-style argument presented in Pascal. He does not argue that it must be rational to accept Christianity, despite the insufficiency of evidence, on the grounds that the resulting sacrifice of worldly pleasure is but a finite loss, whereas eternal happiness represents an infinite gain. Second, it seems that the pragmatist's appeal to self-interest is at odds with the teaching of the New Testament, and hence also with the orthodox view of Christianity held by Kierkegaard. And finally, there is ample textual evidence indicating that Kierkegaard took a very dim view of prudential reasoning. In the authorship, prudence is always set in opposition to faith.[56]

As these concerns have a direct bearing on the plausibility of my thesis, I shall address each of them briefly before proceeding. First, although Kierkegaard does not present a wager-style argument, it does not follow that there is not a pragmatic argument to be found in the authorship. Broadly construed, pragmatism is an attempt to expand the limits of rationality from the point of view of practical considerations. It has taken various forms in the writings of Pascal, Kant, and William James. Though Kierkegaard's view is admittedly not identical with any of these formulations, I believe it can be shown that he holds a place within this larger tradition of pragmatism in religious thought.

Second, it would be a mistake to suppose that the notion of self-interest is at odds with the teaching of the New Testament, or with Kierkegaard's orthodox interpretation of the latter. According to the gospel of Matthew, for example, Jesus is reported to have spoken this way:

> For whosoever will save his life shall lose it: and whosoever will lose his life for my sake shall find it. For what is a man profited, if he shall gain the whole world, and lose his own soul? Or what shall a man give in exchange for his soul?[57]

Here, the founder of Christianity himself encourages his disciples to consider their own interests in the matter of salvation. Similarly, Kierkegaard contends that only those individuals with an "infinite passionate interest" in the possibility of eternal happiness are eligible for this reward.[58] Every individual must come to terms with the question of human mortality. This question, if it is to be meaningful, must be framed in the first person singular: given that I will someday die, what does the possibility of an eternal happiness mean to me?[59] To the extent that I fail to address this question as an interested individual, I do not address it at all.[60]

And finally, Kierkegaard and Climacus frequently use two expressions, *Forstandighed* and *Klogskab*, both of which are translated into English as "prudence." It is clear from the contexts in which these words appear that they pick out a very specific attitude, one characterized by caution and reserve.[61] The prudent man (*den Forstandige*) "feels his way with the understanding in the realm of the probable, and finds God where the probabilities are favorable."[62] This attitude is sharply contrasted with that of faith: "The probable is so little to the taste of a believer that he fears it most of all, since he well knows that when he clings to probabilities it is because he is beginning to lose his faith."[63] It is not prudent to be Christian. Kierkegaard expresses this by saying that faith lies precisely in the realm of the improbable.[64]

According to this narrow construal of the word, prudence suggests something very different from pragmatism. For the latter does not avoid risk, but provides a practical justification for taking risks in view of actual or expected consequences. Thus Kierkegaard says that in Christendom, where people live in the relaxed notion that salvation is a foregone conclusion, it is hardly a prudent thing to want to sacrifice everything in the name of Christianity.[65] Yet, it is precisely "the terror of eternity [that] can oblige and also motivate a human being to venture in such a decisive way and justify his actions."[66]

What then is Kierkegaard's pragmatist faith? As the quotation in the last paragraph suggests, his view bears a strong resemblance to that of William James. But there are important differences as well. I shall start then by putting forward what I take to be a noncontroversial account of James's view, which will be our philosophical framework for understanding Kierkegaard.

In his celebrated defense of religious faith, James challenges the view of reason (and rationality) implicit in the evidentialist view of his day.[67] Evidentialism is a prescriptive doctrine, which says that a person ought to believe only those propositions for which there is sufficient evidential warrant. Quoting W. K. Clifford, James sums up this view in the following way: "It is wrong always, everywhere, and for everyone, to believe anything upon insufficient evidence."[68] In opposition to this view, James questions the assumption that only evidential considerations should determine whether or not it is rational to believe. He argues that there are clear cases where it is rational to accept a belief on the basis of nonevidential considerations; that interest and passion may, under certain circumstances, provide legitimate bases for belief. "Our passional nature," writes James, "not only lawfully may, but must, decide an option between propositions, whenever it is a genuine option that cannot by its nature be decided on intellectual grounds" (20).

Even the most hard-nosed empiricist, whose inquiry is regulated by the dual principle of seeking truth and avoiding error, is not free from the influence of passion. For whether one gives priority to acquiring true beliefs or avoiding false ones is itself a passionate affirmation of desire (25). One may say, "Better go without belief forever than believe a lie" (25). Or one may prefer to run the risk of believing falsely, and thereby avail one-self of certain truths whose realization would be precluded by an overly cautious attitude (24–25). But whichever attitude one finally adopts, one must remember that these are "in any case only expressions of our passional life" (25).

If James is right, then Clifford's commitment to evidentialism is merely an expression of his passional life. It reflects his personal prefer-ence for a more cautious methodology. However, James adds to this a fur-ther argument designed to undercut the ethics of belief position. For Clif-ford not only expresses a preference for the evidentialist rule of thinking, he argues that it ought to take precedence over all others. To this James replies that any "rule of thinking which would absolutely prevent [him] from acknowledging certain kinds of truth if those kinds of truth were really there, would be an irrational rule" (31–32). The trouble with Clif-ford's view is not that it recommends a cautious attitude in matters of belief, but that it recommends this attitude across the board.

James is the first to concede that the "dispassionately judicial intel-lect" ought to be our ideal in purely theoretical matters (27). But he also recognizes that human beings think and act in a wide variety of situations, and that it is necessary to take into account the practical implications of employing a certain rational standard of evidence in a particular context. What counts as an acceptable standard of rationality in science may well give rise to undesirable results when applied to a wide range of practical situations.[70]

Consider the practical situation described in the following scenario. A person is lost in an underground cave. She has only a lantern and a lim-ited supply of fuel. In her wandering, she comes upon an exit. It is not known to her whether this exit leads back to the surface or whether it leads even deeper into the labyrinth. The hypothesis (p) that the exit leads to the surface has just as much evidential support as the rival hypothesis $(-p)$ that it does not lead to the surface. There is no opportunity to gather further evidence, and it will not be long before her light is spent. If she believes that p, acts on p, and p is true, then she will be rescued. If she believes that

-*p*, acts on -*p*, and -*p* is true, then her prospects for survival will be diminished. Her failure to decide in this situation would be the practical equivalent of rejecting *p* and accepting -*p*.

Our unhappy explorer finds herself confronted with what James describes as a "genuine option."[71] She is confronted with a choice between two 'live' hypotheses, *p* and -*p*, which is 'momentous' because it involves a question of life and death, and 'forced' because even the failure to decide commits her to one of the options. What would be the most rational course of action in this situation? To follow Clifford's ethic, it would seem to be incumbent upon our explorer to suspend judgment. However, given the practical advantages of believing that *p*, would it be rational for her to suspend judgment in the matter? In view of the practical constraints of the case, suspending judgment would surely be irrational. Strict adherence to the evidentialist rule of thinking would be no less than suicidal.

Because we affirm that prompt rescue is a more desirable end than perishing (or being trapped in the bowels of a cave for an indefinite period of time), and because we affirm the general principle that an act is rational if it conduces to desirable ends (and irrational if it gives rise to undesirable ones), then in this case we must affirm that the belief that *p* would indeed be rational. The pragmatist view assumes that rational agents always pursue their interests whenever this is feasible. Moreover, it assumes that in certain practical situations where cognitive reason cannot decide an issue one way or the other, and where a decision is nevertheless forced, there must be some recourse to a procedure of rational deliberation which assures us that there is warrant for the course of action we take.

Should we conclude, then, that people may generally believe whatever they like, regardless of what the evidence indicates? Though this is often thought to be the upshot of James's argument, it is an uncharitable reading at best (24–27). For James does not say that we should ignore relevant evidence, or that it is sometimes advisable to put the question of truth aside (25–26). The pragmatist argument does not set utility against evidence. The point is simply that evidential considerations alone do not always provide the best indication of where truth lies, and so should not constitute the only grounds on which our beliefs may be justified. Nor does the pragmatist argument provide a rational warrant for wishful thinking or self-deception. James is concerned only with cases where cognitive evidence is not decisive; and then only with a certain subclass of such cases, dealing with important issues of ethics and religion.

Like James, Kierkegaard stresses the essentially passional nature of belief and doubt. In the *Fragments*, he explains that belief and doubt are not "two kinds of knowledge that can be defined in continuity with each other, for . . . they are opposite passions."[72] To the skeptical mind, it is better to risk the loss of truth than to be in error.[73] And so the skeptic wills to remain in a state of suspended belief (*isostheneia, epochē*).[74] The believer, on the other hand, thinks it is better to risk the chance of being in error than to suffer the loss of truth. But whether one finally decides to be a believer or a skeptic is not so much a conclusion [*Slutning*] as it is a resolution [*Beslutning*],[75] an expression of will.[76] As James puts the point:

> When we stick to it that there *is* truth . . . we do so with our whole nature, and resolve to stand or fall by the results. The sceptic with his whole nature adopts the doubting attitude; but which of us is the wiser, Omniscience only knows.[77]

When the skeptic backs the field against the religious hypothesis, he stakes just as much as the believer does. The issue is not one of intellect versus passion, "it is only intellect with one passion laying down its law."[78]

Kierkegaard does not deny that there is a proper place for dispassionate or objective inquiry. He recognizes that it is generally advisable to believe statements about history when the available evidence supports their truth, that is, when the probabilities are favorable. However, he questions whether objectivity provides an appropriate model for thinking about important issues of ethics and religion.

The objective mode of inquiry is characterized primarily by an attitude of disinterestedness.[79] This is not to say that the scholar and the scientist have no interest in the truth of the statements they make. As James points out: "The most useful investigator, because the most sensitive observer, is always he whose eager interest in one side of the question is balanced by an equally keen nervousness lest he be deceived."[80] However, it is only truth as technically verified that interests the scholarly or scientific mind. "Purely intellectual striving," he points out, "is occupied solely with discovering the truth."[81] The truth of truths might present itself in merely affirmative form, and the objective inquirer would decline to touch it.[82]

Consider the question of death. The objective inquirer affirms the truth of the statement that death is a natural and inevitable part of the human life-cycle. But an objective interest in the question of what it means to die is purely clinical, and the knowledge it yields is of an impersonal nature. We might say that the objective inquirer knows in general what it means to die. Kierkegaard himself admits to having such knowledge.[83] But, he adds, it does not follow that he has therefore understood death:

> I can by no means regard death as something I have understood. Before I pass over to universal history . . . it seems to me that I had better think about this, lest existence mock me, because I had become so learned . . . that I had forgotten to understand what will someday happen to me as to every human being–sometime, nay, what am I saying: suppose death were so treacherous as to come tomorrow![84]

To understand death is not merely to have an intellectual grasp of a medical condition, it is rather a process of coming to terms with one's anxiety over the uncertainty of death. But this can only be done subjectively.

Subjectivity is a passionate concern for one's own existence, and there is no single idea that does more to heighten this concern than the threat of death. The move from objectivity to subjectivity is a move from the general and the abstract to the particular, concrete situation of the individual.[85] Whereas the objective inquirer is concerned with death in general, the subjective inquirer is concerned with the meaning of death for his own life. Anyone who has not addressed the problem of death passionately, as an interested individual, has not properly addressed it at all.

In the realm of subjectivity, it is not merely having a true belief that is important; it is also a question of the value one places on its being true. Consider, for example, the question of immortality. Whereas the objective inquirer is concerned solely with the question of its truth, the subjective inquirer is also concerned with the question of whether it is good, or would be good if it did exist. This is a decision which properly rests with the subject who is concerned about his own immortality.[86] Since it is a question which does not have a decisive objective answer,[87] Kierkegaard reasons that it not only lawfully may, but must be answered in that personal passion which is infinitely interested in an eternal happiness.

It is precisely the question of death, and the possibility of overcoming death, that Christianity throws into sharp relief. Christian revelation presents the existing individual with a genuine option. This option is entertained by Johannes Climacus, who supposes that there awaits him an eternal happiness, a highest good, and that Christianity proposes itself as the sole condition for the attainment of that good.[88]

Climacus is fully prepared to acknowledge the possibility that Christianity is true.[89] This follows from his exposition of the absolute paradox, which shows that theoretical reason cannot effectively decide the truth or falsity of revelation. As a result, purely evidential considerations warrant neither the acceptance nor the rejection of Christianity. It is, of course, only if Christianity is true that anything Climacus does will bear on the attainment of eternal happiness. But if Christianity is true, then he will attain that highest reward only by becoming a believer. Therefore, as we have seen, the venture to believe may be validated on practical grounds.

The encounter with the absolute paradox brings out a basic tension within the concept of rationality itself. Kierkegaard characterizes this tension, the conflict between pure and practical reason, as the absurd:

> Quite simply, the absurd is this: that I, a rational being, must act in the situation where my understanding [and] my reflection say to me: You can just as well do the one thing as the other, where my understanding and reflection say to me: You cannot act—that I nevertheless must act.[90]

The rationality of belief is usually determined by examining the relation of the belief to the evidence in its support, while the rationality of actions is usually determined by reference to the actual or expected consequences. But for Kierkegaard, as for James, belief choices are actions, and so the criteria of rationality that apply to actions apply to beliefs as well.[91] Thus he affirms that, as a rational being, he must believe despite the insufficiency of evidence. As a genuine option, the decision to believe in Christianity is properly decidable in the realm of interest and passion.

Because we affirm that an eternal happiness is more desirable than eternal lostness, and because we affirm the principle that an act is rational if it conduces to desirable ends (and irrational if it gives rise to undesirable ones), we must affirm that belief in Christianity is in fact rational on practical grounds. As Kierkegaard says, the terror of eternity can motivate an individual to venture in a decisive way and also justify his actions. Where the realization of an infinite good (salvation) depends on personal action, he affirms that faith based on desire is certainly a lawful and possibly an indispensable thing: "A final hour is coming, the hour of death. Christ promises you an infinite good, the blessedness of heaven. Would you dispense with that for something else? Well, then choose him."[92]

If the foregoing is an accurate account of the reasoning which underlies the philosophical portion of Kierkegaard's authorship, then in what sense does it differ from that of other pragmatists, most notably James? To answer this question, we must return to the concept of sin and the way that concept functions in Kierkegaard's theologically grounded critique of reason.

It is sin, not merely the discrepancy of the finite and the infinite, that is central to Kierkegaard's critique of reason. Sin is the decisive expression for that which separates human beings from God. In so far as reason represents the very highest achievement of human nature, asserting itself in its totality, it is also the highest expression of human sinfulness. Because human beings suffer from the noetic effects of the fall, it is impossible for the unaided reason to discover the ultimate truth about human existence. This can only be revealed through divine agency.

Assuming that a revelation has occurred, what are human beings to make of it? The main problem with the objective approach to Christianity, as that approach is exemplified in historical and philosophical modes of inquiry, is that it tries to make revelation conform to the standards of human reason. But this is, at bottom, an anti-Christian stance. By attempting to bring the paradox within the sphere of human knowledge, the objective inquiry overlooks the decisive category of sin.[93] It fails to see that revelation does not present itself as an object for human knowledge. Rather, it is an indirect form of communication that provides an occasion for existing individuals to realize that they are in error, and that the standards by which they measure ultimate reality are inadequate. As Kierkegaard explains:

> Suppose that a revelation . . . must be a mystery, and that its sole and sufficient mark is precisely that it is a mystery. . . . Suppose it were after all a blessed thing, critically situated in the extreme press of existence, to sustain a relation to this mystery without understanding it, merely as a believer. Suppose Christianity never intended to be understood; suppose that, in order to express this, and to prevent anyone from entering upon the objective way, it has declared itself to be the paradox. Suppose it wished to have significance only for existing individuals in inwardness, in the inwardness of faith. . . . Suppose it therefore accentuates existence so decisively that the individual becomes a sinner, Christianity the paradox, existence the period of decision."[94]

The absolute paradox sets the stage for this decision by shifting the issue away from the intellectual (objectivity) to the realm of interest and passion (subjectivity). Revelation is not a logical contradiction, but a mystery which claims to hold the solution to the riddle of human existence. It does not present itself as an object for scientific scrutiny, but as the point of departure for a new life. It does this by foreclosing on the objective way, by forcing the individual into himself, into the realm of subjectivity, where the decision must be made.[95]

Revelation addresses itself to the passionate nature of human beings. It enables us to reach a decision by giving us the condition: the recognition of sin, our separateness from God, and our inability to discover God through the unaided intellect.[96] Sin is therefore "the decisive expression for the religious mode of existence."[97] Its acknowledgement is the condition for conversion, in which the individual comes to see self and world not from the point of view of reason as supreme, but from the point of view of reason as untruth.[98]

To overcome paradox, one must do more than recognize the practical value of believing. What is required is an act (or attitude) of repentance.[99] Repentance is the act of self-renouncing, the act of giving up our claims about the superiority of reason. To the extent that we try to penetrate the mystery of revelation through historical or philosophical inquiry, in which we take ourselves to be in a position to present conclusive evidences and arguments, we only reaffirm our sinfulness. It is only through repentance that we begin to move toward the recognition that we are saved by grace alone. In the recognition of sin we must acknowledge Christ as our saviour, without whom we are eternally lost.[100]

But nothing that has been said here diminishes the fact that Christianity presents the existing individual with a genuine option, or that it may be rational to accept the verdict of revelation and seek salvation through faith. From the point of view of an infinite passionate interest, the absurd is not the absurd, for faith transforms it.[101] Revelation does not destroy reason, rather it requires that the individual acknowledge the limits of reason and accept revelation as pointing the way to a higher truth. In this way, reason is made to honor faith.[102]

The picture of Kierkegaard that emerges from this study is quite different from that commonly found in secondary literature. In support of this picture I have focused on what I take to be the two main purposes underlying Kierkegaard's philosophical writings. On the one hand, he puts forward a theological critique of reason, the highest expression of which is the self-sufficient, sterile ideal of objective inquiry. To this end, he attempts to show that Christianity rests on the absolute paradox, and that all attempts at explaining revelation within the finite categories of human reason are doomed to fail. Kierkegaard does not conclude from this, however, that it must be irrational to become Christian. For what the absolute paradox reveals is a basic tension within the concept of rationality itself: the conflict between pure and practical reason. Whereas purely evidential considerations do not warrant the rationality of becoming a believer, there are important practical considerations that render the decision to believe perfectly rational. There is no compelling reason why we should, under the circumstances, limit our decision to the evidence.

This brings us to Kierkegaard's second purpose, namely, to show that faith requires personal action. Though we are saved by grace, this is not something settled and completed once and for all.[103] The decision to believe in Christianity must be "related to a striving," an active appropriation of the truth.[104] To believe in Christianity is to commit oneself passionately to thinking and acting in accordance with the ideal Christian pattern as depicted in the doctrinal narratives of the New Testament. Revelation does not aim at increasing our knowledge or enlightening our intellects, but rather at motivating an existential decision and giving us practical guidance. It calls the individual back to existence and ethics where true Christianity resides.[105]

Kierkegaard thus aptly characterizes faith as a venture.[106] It is a venture in the sense that the decision to believe must be undertaken without objective assurances. In faith, the believer stakes his entire existence on the mere possibility of an eternal happiness. To become a Christian is "to risk everything, to invest absolutely everything in the venture."[107] With respect to the question of whether to become a believer, practical considerations must be decisive.[108]

The pragmatist proposal has two advantages as an interpretation of the Kierkegaardian view of faith. First, it avoids the sort of criticism that the irrationalist interpretation invites. Rather than portraying the believer as one who embraces nonsense, the pragmatist view affirms that we are free to try to achieve by practical means what cannot be achieved otherwise. Second, and finally, it accords well with the Christian intention of the authorship, in so far as it provides the believer with a rationale for the pursuit of what he takes to be an answer to his absolute concern: the possibility of an eternal happiness in the face of inevitable death.

4

Revelation and History

The historical aspect of revelation introduces certain complications into the dialectic of Christian faith. On the one hand, theologians recognize the historical manifestation of God as prerequisite for faith and salvation; while on the other hand, they also recognize that a natural concern for historical accuracy may come into direct conflict with the requirements of obedient discipleship. This issue is addressed by Kierkegaard (Climacus) in the *Fragments* and *Postscript,* where it is argued that a historical point of departure is necessary for Christian faith, but that historical inquiry is at best inconclusive and at worst positively harmful for faith. In this chapter I shall examine the arguments underlying this view.

THE HISTORICAL

The originating concern of the *Fragments* is expressed in the following tripartite question, which appears on the title page: "Can a historical point of departure be given for an eternal consciousness; how can such a point of departure be of more than historical interest; can an eternal happiness be built on historical knowledge?" The first part of this question asks whether it is possible for an individual who is located in history to become conscious of something eternal. The second part asks whether the historical event of learning about the eternal can have more than mere historical interest for the individual. The third part asks whether it is possible for such an individual to base his salvation on what he has learned about a historical event. These questions are aimed at elucidating the relationship between eternal truth and the contingent historical context in which that truth is allegedly communicated to human beings.

61

Kierkegaard begins this discussion, as we have seen, by contrasting two different ways of answering these questions: the Socratic and the Christian. There is no real difficulty from the Socratic point of view, since it is supposed that the learner possesses the truth already and can recover it via introspection. The Socratic teacher is therefore incidental to the process of discovery. But so is the moment of discovery, since the learner is presumably capable of discovering the truth at any given moment.

The Socratic position is developed along the lines of the Platonic theory of recollection described in the *Meno*. In that dialogue, a slave boy who has never had any schooling is questioned by Socrates about a geometric problem, and with some prompting he is able to arrive at the correct answer. The demonstration is intended to make the point that we possess knowledge in the form of a latent memory that can be brought to consciousness by a process of questioning. The slave boy must only be reminded of what he already knows. This theory is proposed as a solution to the conundrum posed at the outset of that dialogue, namely, that "a person cannot possibly seek what he knows, and, just as impossibly, he cannot seek what he does not know, for what he knows he cannot seek, since he knows it, and what he does not know he cannot seek, because, after all, he does not even know what he is supposed to seek."[1]

By contrast, the Christian view says that prior to revelation the learner does not and cannot possess the truth, and hence that he cannot merely recover it via introspection. The Christian teacher not only brings the truth to the learner but also the condition for grasping it, and is therefore necessary to the process of discovery. Moreover, the moment of discovery is decisive, since the teacher must enter history to deliver the truth. The Christian teacher must therefore bring both the truth and the condition for understanding that truth. It follows that such a teacher cannot be a Socrates, for Socrates is not so much a teacher as a stimulus for the individual's recovery (recollection) of the truth.[2]

But there is another more important sense in which the teacher cannot be a Socrates, since the logic of revelation makes it clear that only one person can effect this teaching. The Christian teacher must be different, then, not only with regard to what he does, but also with regard to who he is. Only God is in a position to erase the absolute difference that separates him from his creatures.[3] This teaching requires no less than that the learner be transformed into "a person of a different quality."[4] The slave boy in the *Meno* does not undergo any such transformation, since he does not assimilate anything essentially different from himself. The Christian model assumes that such an assimilation must be the case, and what that difference is, is a divine gift.

One further point of clarification can be made concerning the role of the Christian teacher. It is possible to distinguish at least two non-Socratic models that explain how the learner acquires the truth. On the first model (M1), the teacher gives the truth in such a manner that the individual must still do something to realize the truth. That is, the truth may be given as a capacity for actualization. It will be seen that once the condition is bestowed, the learner is placed in a situation that formally resembles the Socratic, in so far as it requires some sort of activity for the actual appropriation of the truth. On the second model (M2), the condition is given as an actualized capacity, that is, the truth is realized in that moment the condition is bestowed.

It is worth noting that a model similar to M2 is also described by Plato in the *Symposium*. Recounting the speech of Diotima of Mantinea, Socrates explains that the man who is truly a lover of beauty, when he has learned to see the beautiful "in the right and regular ascent, suddenly will have revealed to him . . . a wondrous vision, beautiful in its nature."[5] Such beauty, we are told, is not to be found "in the guise of a face or of hands or any other portion of the body, nor as a particular description or piece of knowledge, nor as existing somewhere in another substance . . ."[6] For what is revealed is the very essence of beauty. We could, of course, explain this in terms of a theory about latent memory. But as George Mavrodes points out, what is described here does not seem to presuppose the theory of recollection. Rather, what it suggests is the possibility of a certain type of experience culminating in a sudden perception, in which a new level of reality is revealed.[7] This new perception of the world might be explained, for example, as the direct result of some divine agency, which causes the individual to see differently. Whether Kierkegaard's discussion presupposes M1, M2 or some variation is a complex question that will be the subject of the next chapter.

In summary, then, the Socratic view maintains that the learner already possesses the truth, and that the historical circumstance of the teaching is an accidental feature. History is merely an occasion for making explicit what is already implicit. The Christian view, by contrast, posits a discontinuity in the temporal order, whereby something essentially different is introduced. The learner cannot proceed by quantitative steps toward the truth. What is required is a qualitative transformation, the condition for which is a divine gift, made possible by God's revelation in history. As a result, the historical circumstance of this teaching takes on decisive importance. Thus the answers to the first two parts of Kierkegaard's question are now clear: an existing individual can indeed become conscious of the eternal in time, and this historical event can have more than mere historical interest, provided that it is the unique historical fact of God's appearance in history.

Kierkegaard refers to the event of God's appearance in history as the "moment." However, this is no ordinary temporal moment, for it is "filled with the eternal":

> A moment such as this is unique. To be sure, it is short and temporal, as the moment is; it is passing, as the moment is, past, as the moment is in the next moment and yet it is decisive, and yet it is filled with the eternal. A moment such as this must have a special name. Let us call it: the *fullness of time*.[8]

Mark C. Taylor points out that Kierkegaard actually speaks of two distinct moments: the "moment of incarnation" and the "moment of faith."[9] But as Paul Müller correctly adds, these are really two aspects of the same moment, since the incarnation is only a reality for those who have faith.[10] Even though it is quite natural to think about the incarnation in a historical context, the fact of God's appearance in time is always a present reality in the context of faith, never a past event. As we shall see, this point has important implications for Kierkegaard's understanding of the historical in relation to faith.

FAITH AND HISTORICAL EVIDENCE

Christian revelation signals a new beginning, the possibility of being related to God in time. Since the only sort of relationship that an existing individual can have to God is a spiritual relationship, the aim of revelation is to effect the kind of inward transformation that makes such a relationship possible. But Kierkegaard points out that historical inquiry is inimical to the spiritual development of the individual. For even though Christianity requires a minimum of historical information, the incarnation is not properly an object for historical knowledge; it is only an object for faith. According to this view, objective inquiry into the credibility of historical evidence is at best inconclusive and at worst a harmful diversion. The answer to the third part of our original question, then, is that one cannot base an eternal happiness on historical evidence.

The irrelevance of historical evidence to faith is expressed in the *Fragments* in the following way:

> Even if the contemporary generation had not left anything behind except these words, "We have believed that in such and such a year the god appeared in the humble form of a servant, lived and taught among us, and then died"–this is more than enough. The contemporary generation would have done what is needful, for this little announcement, this world-historical *nota bene,* is enough to become an occasion for someone who comes later, and the most prolix report can never in all eternity become more for the person who comes later.[11]

What this suggests is that there is really only one way to acquire faith: through a personal encounter with Jesus Christ.[12] This line of reasoning is continued in the *Postscript,* where Kierkegaard puts forward a series of arguments against the evidentialist view. He begins by pointing out the decisive significance that the Bible has for historical scholarship:

> When one raises the historical question of the truth of Christianity, or of what is and is not Christian truth, the Scriptures at once present themselves as documents of decisive significance. The historical inquiry therefore first concentrates upon the Bible.[13]

There are two forms this type of inquiry can take. The first is purely philological. The philologist is concerned only to give the text its most accurate form possible. This is, in Kierkegaard's view, a perfectly legitimate and meaningful task. He says that "philological scholarship is absolutely within its rights," and that he "yields to none in profound respect for that which science consecrates."[14]

The aim of the philological inquiry differs, however, from that of the critical theologian. Though the latter agrees with the philologist that textual criticism is an important and worthwhile task, he wants to go further. The critical theologian applies the scholarly-scientific method to the Holy Scriptures, and "when he has completed his task (and until then he keeps us in suspense, but holds this prospect before us) he draws the conclusion: *ergo,* now you can base your eternal happiness on these writings."[15] What the critical theologian fails to understand, however, is that historical inquiry, which is concerned with empirical matters, is wholly inappropriate as a means of justifying faith. At best, it can yield only 'approximate' results. Moreover, closer examination reveals that critical theology and faith are concerned with entirely incommensurable objects. Whereas the critical theologian asks whether the books of the Bible are authentic, whether they stand in an integral relation to each other, and whether their authors are trustworthy, the concern of faith is whether they are the product of divine inspiration, whether they truly represent the word of God. The most that the critical theologian can assert is that "it is as if every letter were inspired."[16]

Kierkegaard affirms the view that all historical facts are contingent, and that because all demonstrations based on empirical evidence employ inductive principles which are themselves only inductively validated, it is "impossible in the case of historical problems to reach an objective decision so certain that no doubt could disturb it."[17] One important point he draws from this is that the amount of error we can tolerate will depend on what is at stake.[18] Where the truth or falsity of what we believe is of no great consequence (apart from the general desire not to hold false beliefs), a small chance of error may well prove negligible. But if one had an infinite passionate interest in the outcome, as might be the case with regard to an eternal happiness, then no possibility of error would be too little to worry about: "In relation to an eternal happiness, and an infinite passionate interest in its behalf (in which latter alone the former can exist), an iota is of importance, of infinite importance."[19] Thus the way of approximation is "essentially incommensurable with an infinite personal interest in an eternal happiness."[20]

The underlying point is that faith requires a kind of certainty that historical inquiry cannot provide. Given that empirical inquiry cannot preclude the possibility of error, it is always possible that further evidence will come to light that will force us to revise our beliefs.[21] What this means is that we are never in a position to make a final decision. As Kierkegaard points out, "new difficulties arise and are overcome, and new difficulties again arise," with the result that the decision is postponed.[22] But faith requires absolute decisiveness and certainty of conviction. The believer must be willing to risk everything, to embrace the uncertainty of his object with the passion of the infinite.[23]

Kierkegaard's claim that an eternal happiness can only be pursued with an infinite passionate interest is crucial, because it points to a deeper concern about the inadequacy of historical inquiry. For even if one could attain empirical certainty with regard to the authenticity of the biblical canon, the task of acquiring and preserving faith would not be helped but hindered, since the proper relationship to Christianity is not one of mere intellectual assent: "Faith does not result simply from a scientific inquiry. . . . On the contrary, in this objective inquiry one tends to lose that infinite personal interestedness in passion which is the condition for faith."[24] Though faith involves giving assent to a proposition about a historical event (the appearance of God in time), it is to be understood primarily as a life-transforming passion. The decision to become a Christian is "an act of freedom, an expression of will,"[25] a resolution to commit oneself to a life of ethical-religious striving.

By acknowledging the uncertainty of his object, the believer does not confess doubt about the correctness of his choice:

> By no means. On this "if" he risks his entire life, he has the courage to meet death, and he has with the passion of the infinite so determined the pattern of his life that it must be found acceptable—*if* there is an immortality. Is any better proof capable of being given for the immortality of the soul?[26]

In view of the emphasis Kierkegaard places on the moral imperative embodied in the Christ-revelation, the language in this passage is strongly suggestive of the reasoning that underlies Kant's moral proof for the existence of God.[27] Kant argues that although moral practice presupposes a belief in both immortality and the existence of God—which are affirmed as postulates of the moral life—the meaning of these beliefs is borne out not by objective evidence, which is lacking, but in the commitment to perfect oneself through a life of moral striving. Similarly, as Kierkegaard points out both in the Climacus writings and in *Practice in Christianity*, belief in the truth of revelation is manifested in the commitment to the task of perfecting oneself in the image of Christ. In this way, the affirmation of God's existence and of one's belief in an eternal happiness is intimately linked with moral practice, or as Kierkegaard frequently expresses it, 'the ethical.'

It is important to note that Kant did not take the result of his 'proof' to be a kind of objective knowledge, but rather a species of personal conviction embodying a moral certainty.[28] As the above-quoted passage suggests, it is precisely a form of personal conviction that grounds the certainty of Kierkegaardian faith, a conviction that is borne out in the individual's personal resolve to follow Christ. It is in this light that we are to understand Kierkegaard's observation that the "conclusion of belief is not so much a conclusion as a resolution, and it is for this reason that belief excludes all doubt."[29]

There are, of course, important differences in the way Kierkegaard and Kant conceive of the role of historical revelation in the process of redemption. One such difference is that Kant goes even further than Kierkegaard by downplaying the historicity of the Christian revelation. As Ronald M. Green points out, Kant denies that we "can draw moral or religious nourishment from historical 'examples' since these attain their power and must always be tested against the indwelling moral concepts of our own reason."[30] Moreover, he rejects the critical theologian's project, arguing that

> Since our moral improvement is the sole condition of eternal life the only way we can find eternal life in any Scripture whatsoever is by putting it there. For the concepts and principles required for eternal life cannot really be learned from anyone else: the teacher's exposition is only the occasion for him to develop them out of his own reason.[31]

In the end, Kant concludes that it is superstition to believe that historical belief is essential to salvation.[32]

Green correctly notes that Christ is not a "midwife who draws out our a priori knowledge," but the divine "judge and savior who in a 'decisive' moment in time redeems the learner from his captivity to sin and error."[33] But this may only be partially right, since Kierkegaard affirms that

> The ethical presupposes that every person knows what the ethical is, and why? Because the ethical demands that every man shall realize it at every moment, but then he surely has to know it. The ethical does not begin with ignorance which is to be changed to knowledge but begins with a knowledge and demands a realization.[34]

This passage appears in the context of a larger discussion about the nature of indirect communication, where he argues that the 'how' of the ethical is not something that can be directly taught or communicated. Kierkegaard affirms that the recognition of a moral imperative as binding on one's life presupposes a kind of knowledge. But how does this apparent endorsement of the theory of recollection fit with the account of teaching presupposed in the Climacus writings?

We have already noted that once the God-man bestows the condition, the learner is in a situation that formally resembles the Socratic. This is confirmed in the following statement: "The teacher, then, is the god himself, who, acting as the occasion, prompts the learner to be reminded that he is untruth and is that through his own fault."[35] Yet this is only part of the picture, for in the very next paragraph it is affirmed that the Christian teacher is also "the god, who gives the condition and gives the truth."[36] What this suggests is that the God-man has a dual role as teacher.[37] On the one hand, he is the uniquely necessary teacher who provides the condition for faith: the consciousness of sin. In this way, he differs from the Socratic midwife, who brings nothing new to the learner. But once the condition is bestowed, the God-man becomes, by his example, the occasion for the learner to be "reminded that he is untruth." In this way, he is very much like the Socratic midwife.

Kierkegaard clearly disagrees with Kant, however, that belief in a historical redeemer is unwarranted superstition. It is by virtue of the fact that revelation occurs in the historical context that the absolute paradox is generated: without the paradox, there would be no passion and no faith. But just as we cannot ignore the historicity of revelation, we must be careful not to give the historical a decisive significance.[38] The appearance of God in history must not be reduced to a "simple historical fact."[39] This has prompted some critics to wonder whether Kierkegaard can legitimately maintain the necessity of belief in a historical savior, while denying the relevance of historical evidence. Kierkegaard's reasoning, as we have seen, is that faith can only be based on a personal encounter with Christ, and that the historicity of revelation merely provides the existing individual an occasion for such an encounter. Yet one might wonder whether this is a sufficient reason for ruling out the relevance of historical evidence altogether. C. Stephen Evans contends that it is not.[40]

Evans begins by pointing out that Christianity requires a commitment to certain historical beliefs. Chief among these is the belief that God has existed in the form of an individual human being. Even if we admit that we cannot prove the truth of this claim, is it really possible to believe that it is true, and yet be entirely indifferent to evidence and arguments to the contrary? The Christian belief in Jesus Christ is a belief with historical content, and as such it cannot be isolated from other historical beliefs. To the extent that "it is important for our information to be historically accurate, how can we avoid a concern for the quality of the historical evidence?"[41]

Evans notes that one reason why Kierkegaard rules out the question of historical evidence is that he wants to prevent faith from becoming a subject of endless scholarly debate.[42] The individual who must decide whether or not to become a Christian "does not have the luxury of waiting for the scholars to reach agreement, which will never happen in any case."[43] Still, Kierkegaard is not logically forced to rule out historical evidence as a supplementary basis for faith, since it does not follow from the admission of such evidence that the decision to believe would thereby be indefinitely postponed. According to Evans, it is quite possible for a believer to claim that

> it is significant that we have as much evidence as we have, and even to admit that some people would not find faith to be possible if they did not have evidence of reasonable, even if not decisive quality, while still properly believing that the decision is not in the end one which scholarship can settle.[44]

Thus, even if we admit that evidential considerations are neither necessary nor sufficient to produce faith, Evans suggests that they may well play an important role in confirming an existing faith. From this perspective, faith makes it possible to appreciate and assess evidence in the proper light, thereby providing the believer with an assurance that his beliefs have not been undermined by various "defeaters."[45] Although the arguments in the *Postscript* are intended to show that one cannot come to faith by way of historical evidence, Evans raises a valid question about whether the existence of faith might not itself supply a context in which that evidence can be relevant.

It is true that one's faith may be confirmed by certain kinds of choices and certain kinds of experiences, such as the act of being a witness to miracles. But Kierkegaard emphatically disagrees with the suggestion that miracles could actually serve as evidence for faith: "The miracle can demonstrate nothing, for if you do not believe him to be who he says he is, then you deny the miracle."[46] This argument, which is entirely consistent with the position taken in the Climacus writings, suggests that historical evidence is superfluous to faith.

If we admit, as Evans does, that faith is properly grounded in "a firsthand experience of Jesus for which historical records serve only as an occasion,"[47] then the subsequent appeal to external evidence could not add meaningfully to one's faith. Such an appeal to evidence would seem to indicate rather that one was losing faith. This point is in fact acknowledged by Evans, who says that "a believer who is troubled by doubt might admit the relevance of historical argument."[48] But the quote from Anti-Climacus clearly suggests that miracles lack evidential value in the traditional sense of what evidence is. On this point, Kierkegaard appears to agree with the judgment of John Stuart Mill that "miracles have no claim whatever to the character of historical facts and are wholly invalid as evidences of any revelation."[49] Miracles are valuable, not because they confirm the truth of one's faith, but because they confirm the fact of one's faith.

Moreover, we have already seen that a faith that is properly grounded is marked by the certainty of moral conviction. Kierkegaardian faith begins by embracing the objective uncertainty of its object with the passion of the infinite. But if this is the case, then Evans's argument for the relevance of historical evidence will not work. For if a believer is so troubled by doubts about the historicity of revelation that he finds it necessary to bolster his faith with external evidence, then it would appear to be circular reasoning to claim that faith must also provide the context in which that evidence is seen to be both reasonable and sufficient.[50] Faith cannot derive meaningful support from evidence that itself is only efficacious in the light of faith. Kierkegaard's original position is more consistent: either the believer is secure in his faith, in which case the appeal to external evidence is superfluous; or else the believer is losing faith, in which case the appeal to external evidence will not help.

A further problem with Evans's argument is the implicit assumption that historical evidence can increase the probability that Christianity is true. Commenting on this point, Brand Blanshard explains: "We may grant that historical research, by seeking independent confirmation of the report of a given gospel may lend a given event a higher probability, but certainty is beyond our grasp."[51] The crucial question is whether Kierkegaard actually makes this assumption.

This brings us to what I believe is Kierkegaard's main reason for rejecting historical evidence as a basis for faith: the absolute paradox. Objectively viewed, the incarnation seems at best highly improbable. It is not the kind of event for which we would expect to have good evidence. But more important, Kierkegaard makes it clear that the object of faith transcends the range of possible human knowledge. To make such an event probable, which is the aim of historical inquiry, would amount to falsifying it. Revelation is not the sort of event about which there can be knowledge, and it is for this reason that all attempts to secure an evidential basis for faith are fundamentally misguided. The truth of Christianity, the efficacy of miracles, the divine inspiration of the biblical authors—all these things depend ultimately upon the authenticity of the Christian revelation. But no amount of historical inquiry can penetrate the essential mystery of God's appearance in time. The incarnation can only be grasped by faith.

Finally, it may be noted that Evans's criticism underestimates the extent to which the discussion in the Climacus writings is framed by the theological concept of obedience. Kierkegaard insists that the paradox does not present itself for judgment by human reason, but is intended rather to be a judgment upon human reason. To take the Christian view, therefore, is to see revelation as absolutely authoritative, and to see the corresponding response of faith as one of trustful obedience. Either revelation is the standard of what is true and false, or else human reason is; but we cannot have it both ways.[52] Given the logic of this argument, Kierkegaard is justified in claiming that the search for historical evidence is incompatible with the claims of revelation.

The foregoing argument is further supported by the discussion in the fifth chapter of the *Fragments,* where it is claimed that historical contemporaneity with the teacher can yield no advantage where faith is concerned. If it were possible to secure a belief in Christianity on grounds external to revelation, then this would give the contemporary eyewitness a natural advantage over one who was born 1800 years later. But since God is not a possible object for human knowledge, then believers at all times in history are on an equal footing with respect to the object of their faith. No advantage can accrue to the eyewitness, for as Kierkegaard points out, if he believes his eyes, then he is deceived, for the god cannot be known directly. Because revelation is not a simple historical fact, it resists all attempts to "naturalize" it.[53] There is no amount of historical evidence that can render the Christian paradox probable.

To deny that historical evidence can be a basis for faith is not, however, to deny that there may be reasons for becoming a Christian. Kierkegaard's demonstrated affinity to what was earlier described as a 'pragmatic tradition' in religious thought points unmistakably toward a legitimate role for objective reasoning in religion. I shall turn now briefly to examine Kierkegaard's relationship to the other major figures in that tradition: Pascal and Kant.

FAITH AND PRACTICAL REASON

Consider the following passage from *Pensees*:

> If there is a God, He is infinitely incomprehensible, since, having neither parts nor limits, He has no affinity to us. We are incapable of knowing either what He is or if He is. This being

so, who will dare to undertake the decision of the question? Not we, who have no affinity to Him.[54]

According to Pascal, there are insufficient evidential grounds on which to support a belief in Christianity, and we must therefore admit that the object of faith is objectively uncertain. Furthermore, we cannot blame Christians for not being able to demonstrate the truth of their religion, for "if they proved it, they would not keep their word; it is in lacking proofs that they are not lacking in sense."[55]

The same points can be found in the *Fragments*, where Kierkegaard affirms both the unknowability of God and the futility of all metaphysical and historical demonstrations of God's existence.[56] With respect to the question of whether God exists, or more specifically, whether God has existed in time, theoretical reason cannot decide one way or the other. It does not follow from this, however, that belief in the truth of the Christian incarnation is impossible. Rather, the point is to call attention to the limits of theoretical reason. Kierkegaard cites with approval Neander's interpretation of Pascal,[57] in which he "correctly points out that Pascal divides the theoretical and the practical in man and established the practical as the highest."[58]

The distinction between practical and theoretical reason becomes the foundation of Pascal's celebrated Wager Argument, which attempts to provide a rational warrant for the acceptance of Christianity. By drawing a distinction between what we know to be true and what we are well advised to believe, Pascal defends a form of practical reasoning that runs as follows: if we wager that God exists, we gain an eternal happiness if we are right and lose little if we are wrong; but if we wager that God does not exist, we gain little if we are right and lose an eternal happiness if we are wrong. The Wager Argument shows that the clear advantage lies with belief, and that the individual who values an eternal happiness is therefore well advised to become a Christian.[59]

The Wager Argument has been attacked by critics as a crass and irreligious form of reasoning. However, the question of whether this criticism is justified is not pertinent to the present discussion, since it has already been noted that Kierkegaard does not put forward a wager-style argument. Though he acknowledges that there are practical reasons for becoming a Christian, he emphasizes that such reasons must be rooted in the recognition of human sinfulness and the profound need for redemption. This position is developed in the context of the individual's personal encounter with the Christ-revelation. By his example, Christ is an occasion for the individual to become aware of his moral shortcomings, and to realize that he is incapable of redeeming himself. The decision to become a disciple must be seen by the individual as a "life-necessity."[60] Kierkegaard himself does not endorse anything that even remotely resembles a rational form of self-insurance.

Nevertheless, the formal similarities between Kierkegaard and Pascal are revealing. Both thinkers affirm that to decide against Christianity is to risk the loss of an eternal happiness, while the decision to believe must be made without the benefit of any objective assurances. Moreover, they agree that Christianity confronts the individual with an option that cannot be decided on theoretical grounds, but requires a practical decision that takes the individual's interest into account; and that it is a forced decision in the sense that to be indifferent, to suspend judgment, is practically equivalent to deciding in the negative.

A similar parallel can be drawn between Kierkegaard and Kant on the rationality of religious belief. However, just as in the case of James and Pascal, these agreements must be appreciated within a context of disagreement. We have already noted that Kant sharply downplays the role of the historical. By contrast, the historicity of revelation is the very cornerstone of Kierkegaard's account of faith. Indeed, he tells us that the difficulty of becoming a Christian is precisely that "every Christian is such only by being nailed to the paradox of having based his eternal happiness upon the relation to something historical."[61] Kant simply fails to see the plausibility of the claim that human sinfulness could warrant an event such as the incarnation. The historical Jesus is transformed by Kant into a moral archetype, and the possibility of human salvation is seen to depend on the exercise of moral reason. This position is further supported by Kant's reinterpretation of the doctrine of original sin as a theory about radical evil in human nature which accounts for our moral failing. Thus whereas Kierkegaard, in line with the orthodox Christian position, denies that human beings can redeem themselves, Kant favors a "qualified human initiative in the process of moral redemption."[62]

But once these very focused disagreements are made clear, larger agreements become evident. First of all, as Green notes, the logic of Kant's position does not rule out the idea that God's intervention in history is required to effect human salvation. But more important, Kierkegaard's understanding of why the God-man is the absolute paradox presupposes Kant's theory of knowledge; and so does his solution.[63] For as Green observes, "it is the whole point of Kant's epistemology to deny that everything we cannot *think* also cannot *be*."[64] This view, which allows Kant to posit the existence of a supreme moral causality underlying events in the world, forms the basis of a practical faith which can be found in Kierkegaard. Because God and immortality are necessary postulates for the human life, Kant argues that it must be rationally permissible to predicate them as existing, thereby reconciling the theoretical with our practical interest. In a resounding affirmation of this view, Kierkegaard explains that

> the only way in which an existing individual comes into rela-
> tion with God, is when the dialectical contradiction brings his
> passion to the point of despair, and helps him to embrace God
> with the "category of despair" (faith). Then the postulate is so
> far from being arbitrary that it is a life-necessity. It is then not
> so much that God is a postulate, as that the existing individual's
> postulation of God is a necessity.[65]

By stressing the centrality of the paradox, Kierkegaard drives a wedge between knowledge and faith, and affirms a practical justification for belief in the historical fact of God's existence. But he does so, as we have seen, by emphasizing human sinfulness and the recognition of our total dependence on divine grace. As Green correctly observes, faith is a postulate for Kierkegaard, "but it is a postulate seized upon in the very depths of moral despair."[66]

Because they delineate sharply between the spheres of faith and knowledge, Kierkegaard and Kant both see the transition to the religious as involving "the willed acceptance of beliefs that have no grounding in 'objective' reality."[67] Faith, which is a category unto itself, can only be reached by a qualitative and volitional 'leap' beyond the sphere of knowledge. It has long been assumed that Kierkegaard's notion of the leap of faith emerged from his reading of Lessing. But as Green shows, Kant also uses this term, in works that were familiar to Kierkegaard, to describe an illegitimate move beyond the limits of reason. Of course, this does not by itself establish the priority of Kant's influence. What makes him the more likely source of Kierkegaard's understanding of the leap is that his account involves one crucial element missing in Lessing's, namely, that the leap stands in a paradoxical relationship to all human knowledge.[68] In this crucial respect, Kant's position is seen to be "far closer to Kierkegaard's thinking than anything found in Lessing."[69]

Apart from the fact that Kant does not extend his practical argument to belief in the historical Christ, there is one other way in which his account differs. For Kierkegaard, the leap of faith is qualified by the concept of grace. Though the decision to believe requires a volitional effort, he denies that the individual can simply will himself into a God-relationship. This raises questions once again about the nature of the human response to divine revelation, and in particular about how the will functions in response to the God-man's bestowal of the condition for faith. It is to this question that we turn in the next chapter.

5

Grace and Will
in the Transition to Faith

Having discussed the logic of Christian revelation and its implications for Kierkegaard's view of faith and history, we turn now to a closer examination of the relationship between grace and will in the transition to faith. Kierkegaard's own pronouncements on this matter are often ambiguous, leading to widely divergent interpretations of his thought. In this chapter I shall examine the problem of grace and will in the light of Kierkegaard's discussion of Christian faith in the Climacus writings and the *Journals and Papers*.

GRACE AND WILL

Kierkegaard frequently stresses that faith is not a natural human faculty but a gift of divine grace, a miracle. In the *Fragments*, it is explained that faith is not an act of will, since all human willing presupposes the possession of a grace-given condition.[1] This view derives further support from the *Papers*, where Kierkegaard advocates the doctrine of *sola gratia*.[2] Yet there are passages in those very same works where he claims that the will plays a constitutive role in faith, both in the ordinary sense of the word,[3] and in the Christian sense.[4] More specifically, he claims that Christian faith requires a free, personal decision to surrender the understanding in the encounter with the God-man.[5] To be a believer in this eminent sense involves a "leap."[6] These remarks indicate that the transition to faith cannot properly be understood apart from the cooperative will of the human agent. The problem has been to articulate the relationship between divine grace and this voluntary human response.

Some commentators have made divine grace the central feature of Kierkegaardian faith. As one author recently put it: "Whether we like it or not, faith enters the world as a miracle and as such resists our attempt to explain it by an appeal to the will."[7] Yet others have stressed Kierkegaard's remarks concerning the constitutive role of the will in faith, and have even criticized him for advocating an untenable form of volitionalism.[8] How are we to account for such radically divergent interpretations? Part of the problem is that Kierkegaard sometimes speaks as though faith presupposes the bestowal of a grace-given condition (*Betingelsen*), while at other times he speaks as though faith is identical with that very condition. It would seem, then, that faith is either a volitional act made possible by a grace-given condition, or else faith is itself a grace-given condition, in which case it is not the result of human volition. It is this type of reasoning, at any rate, that underlies much of the current debate concerning the relationship between grace and will in Kierkegaardian faith.

One strategy is simply to deny that Kierkegaard equates faith with the condition. There is, however, strong textual evidence to the contrary. In the *Papers*, for example, he explicitly says that "the teacher must also give the *condition*–(faith is the condition)."[9] This is supported by the following passage from the *Fragments*, in which Kierkegaard describes the optimal encounter between the understanding and the paradox:

> It occurs when the understanding and the paradox happily encounter each other in the moment, when the understanding steps aside and the paradox gives itself, and the third something, the something in which this occurs . . . is that happy passion to which we shall now give a name. . . . We shall call it *faith*. This passion, then, must be that above-mentioned condition that the paradox provides.[10]

It is significant that Kierkegaard describes faith here as a kind of passion. As George Stengren points out, he was certainly aware that the Greek and Latin roots of the word *passion* denote an action being done to a subject, and he probably had this etymological connection in mind when he described Christian faith in terms of passion.[11] This point would seem to support the view that divine grace is both necessary and sufficient for faith.

The view that Kierkegaard equates faith with the condition is also presupposed in the accounts of many representative scholars. C. Stephen Evans observes that according to Climacus "faith is 'the condition' that makes belief possible, and he claims that this condition is a gift to the believer from God."[12] And Louis P. Pojman, whose reading of Kierkegaard is in other ways very different from that of Evans, describes faith as "the necessary condition for being able to entertain the proposition that God has come into existence."[13] Now according to our initial statement of the problem, the identification of faith with the condition would seem to commit these commentators to the idea that faith is not an act of will. Yet Evans claims that "no individual can achieve the state of faith merely by his own efforts."[14] This certainly implies that some human effort is involved in faith, since it is construed here as a kind of achievement. And according to Pojman, who ascribes to Kierkegaard a form of volitionalism, "the will is still free to assent or reject the proposition once faith makes a decision possible. Human freedom is still operative in the midst of grace."[15]

The question is whether we can reconcile the claim that faith involves a personal decision with the claim that faith is a gift of grace. The answer appears to depend on the manner in which the condition is given. Evans suggests that faith "is not produced by an act of will on the part of the believer, but rather is an act of God. All that the believer can will to do is to be open to God's gift of grace."[16] This might lead one to suppose that for Evans the transition to faith does not involve an act of will on the part of the individual.[17] But Evans rejects this interpretation, affirming that the individual's decision to accept or reject God's revelation of human sinfulness "determines whether he can choose to accept the gift of faith that God offers in Christ."[18] Thus Evans does see a role for the will in the acquisition of faith. The view put forward by Pojman, on the other hand, clearly distinguishes between faith given as a potential for actualization, and faith given as an actualized condition. For Pojman faith is a grace-given potential that requires an actualizing response from the human side; it is the condition that enables the individual's free, personal decision to believe in the incarnation. In this way, he affirms that although the acquisition of faith is not an act of human will, the exercise of faith certainly is. As Pojman points out: "Those who receive the condition (the capacity to believe) as a gift must still exercise their wills and make a 'leap of faith.'"[19] Here the bestowal of the condition is necessary but not sufficient for the exercise of faith.

Pojman wants to avoid the claim that faith is simply given as an actualized condition, since that interpretation would seem to undermine the very element of human freedom that is so central to Kierkegaard's understanding of the human response to divine revelation. To assume that the human will plays no part in faith is to assume that the salutary acts of human agents are not their own. This goes to the heart of the traditional theological problem of grace and freedom.

Many theologians, including Kierkegaard, have insisted that human agents are totally dependent on grace, even to the extent that grace can only be received if its very reception is conditioned by grace. It might be suggested that some measure of human freedom is preserved even in this relationship, since the agent presumably has the ability to refuse grace. But, to paraphrase Karl Rahner, how can we maintain that an agent is free in this salutary act and has the ability to refuse the grace offered for such an act, and yet at the same time requires interior grace for the latter?[20] Kierkegaard is acutely aware of this problem. In the appendix to the third chapter of the *Fragments*, he points out that offense at the paradox, which appears to originate in the individual's understanding, really originates in the paradox itself. Thus, properly understood, "all offense is a suffering."[21] And though he goes on to claim that "taking offense" is a human act, and not merely an event in a human life,[22] there is a sense in which even this act is conditioned by God's grace. I do not mean to suggest by this that the doctrine of *sola gratia* inevitably commits one to some form of determinism. Certainly, Kierkegaard did not believe that this doctrine rendered all human striving toward salvation redundant or impossible. What he did believe was that all such striving is in some (yet to be defined) sense conditioned by divine grace. In a crucial passage in the *Papers*, he writes:

> But no one can give himself faith; it is a gift of God I must pray for. Fine, but then I myself can pray, or must we go farther and say: No, praying (consequently praying for faith) is a gift of God which no man can give to himself; it must be given to him. And what then? Then to pray aright must again be given to me so that I may rightly pray for faith, etc. There are many, many [envelopings]–but there must still be one point or another where there is a halt at subjectivity . . . unless we want to have fatalism.[23]

The problem for us is to articulate the point at which subjectivity (the will) becomes operative. It should be evident that any interpretation that fails to account for the role of the will in the transition to faith will fall short of the mark.

In this respect, the interpretation put forward by Pojman has the advantage that it attempts to specify the volitional aspect of faith. But his formulation of that account is problematic. For what does it mean to have an unactualized faith? Surely this is an implication of the position he advocates, since it is assumed that faith is the condition that makes belief in the incarnation possible, and yet there is no guarantee that the individual will make use of that gift once it is bestowed. It might be replied that the gift is not faith itself, but rather a capacity to have faith. Indeed, this idea is suggested in Pojman's description of the organ of faith as "a capacity for receiving the truth."[24] The problem, however, is that he identifies faith with this grace-given condition or capacity.

It is implausible to suppose that an individual can be said to have faith in the fullest sense without believing. To have faith in the Christian sense means, among other things, that one believes in the truth that is revealed in Christ; that one chooses to make Christ the object of one's ethical-religious striving. At least, this seems to be the view that is assumed in the Climacus writings. Perhaps it will be suggested that what Kierkegaard means by 'having faith' is simply being in the possession of a capacity to believe in the truth of the incarnation. But Kierkegaard's language clearly suggests that one either has faith, and consequently believes in Christ, or else one does not.[25] And though he says in the *Fragments* that faith is the condition for believing in the incarnation, he does not describe it as an unactualized potential. That is, Kierkegaard does not say that one can have faith and yet not believe. Conversion, as it is described in the *Fragments*, involves the movement from unbelief to belief. But this aspect of the transition to faith is not fully explained by an account that distinguishes between the moment at which faith (the condition) is bestowed and the moment at which the individual resolves to become a disciple.

As M. Jamie Ferreira points out, Pojman's account of the acquisition of faith agrees with the antivolitionalist position, which also claims that faith is a grace-given condition.[26] The difference between their accounts can be seen in the fact that the antivolitionalist equation of faith with the condition removes the further need for human activity in the transition to faith, while Pojman supplements his position with a volitionalist account of the leap. But the problem with this move, as Ferreira correctly points out, is that by

> locating the decision or leap *after* the acquisition of faith, it fails to do justice to the free, responsible, activity ingredient *in* the acquisition of faith which, I suggest, is the point of Climacus's references to the happy passion of faith in which the understanding *sets itself aside.*(68)

Ferreira puts forward an alternative interpretation that purports to explain the role of free, responsible human agency in the acquisition of faith, but which attempts to do so "in terms other than decision" (69). That account, which we shall now consider, begins with a closer look at the nature of the 'condition.'

FAITH CONDITIONED BY GRACE

The salient difference between the Christian model of teaching and the Socratic is that the latter presupposes the doctrine of recollection: that the learner already possesses the condition (the truth), which can be recalled to thought with the assistance of a teacher. In the Socratic view, the teacher is an accidental feature of the learning process, since the learner is already in possession of the truth. In Christianity, by contrast, the truth is not immanently possessed by the learner; it must come from the outside. Here the teacher is said to be necessary in the sense that he must provide the truth as well as the condition for grasping the truth.[27] This gift effects a "turning around" of the individual toward the truth,[28] a rebirth,[29] which is a qualitative transformation.

According to Ferreira, the transformation that is the condition for understanding the truth can be interpreted in either of two ways: either as "the conferral of a potentiality to be actualized, a capacity to be exercised,"[30] which corresponds to M1 described earlier, or as "the conferral of an actualized ability or capacity" (70), which corresponds to M2 (see page 63). The latter, as we have seen, is the antivolitionalist interpretation, according to which the gift is a necessary and sufficient condition for faith. Although this account differs from the Socratic, "it deprives the notion of a 'leap' (or more precisely, a free transition) of any content" (71). The advantage of M1 is that it allows for the "possibility of giving some content to the notion of free, responsible activity in the acquisition of faith . . . for it implies that one still has to do something by way of response to the condition" (71). This is the model on which Ferreira builds her account.

The key to this account lies in understanding the precise nature of the difference between the Christian and Socratic positions. It is explained that "from the Socratic point of view I possess the condition and now can will it. But if I do not possess the condition . . . then all my willing is of no avail, even though, once the condition is given, that which was valid for the Socratic is again valid."[31] The manner in which one wills this is explained in the following way:

> If the learner were himself the condition for understanding the truth, then he merely needs to recollect, because the condition

for understanding the truth is like being able to ask about it–
the condition and the question contain the conditioned and the
answer.[32]

Once possessed, the character of the condition as given by the teacher
seems to be the same as the condition possessed eternally–a question containing an answer.

Assuming that the possession of the understanding of the truth is not
itself a sufficient condition for realizing that understanding, "one could
expect that in the Christian parallel the god-given condition for understanding the truth would be a condition *for* a realized or actualized understanding (a necessary but not sufficient condition)."[33] It may be true, as
Kierkegaard says, that "the god gave the follower the condition to see it
and opened for him the eyes of faith,"[34] but our free activity is still
required. Thus faith involves the agent's actualization of a bestowed capacity. With regard to those texts that equate the 'condition' with faith, Ferreira offers the following explanation. Though Kierkegaard says that the
paradox provides the mutual understanding in which the understanding
steps aside and the paradox gives itself,[35] it does not follow from this that
we are given that understanding whether or not we want it. Indeed, if we
interpret that mutual understanding "along the lines of a question which
contains an answer, there is room, and need of, a transition to a realized
understanding. Since the question contains the answer it is understandable
that Climacus could apply the term 'faith' to both."[36]

As it stands, this analysis offers just the right account of the dialectic
between grace and will in the acquisition of faith. Though other commentators have presupposed a similar model of the transition to faith, Ferreira's elucidation of it brings a new level of conceptual clarity to the current debate. What is truly original about Ferreira's account, though, is her
analysis of how the will functions in response to the condition. It is to this
part of her analysis that we now turn.

REEXAMINING THE LEAP OF FAITH

We have seen that Kierkegaard uses the term *willing* to describe what it is
that the Socratic learner does when prompted to recollect. But, as Ferreira
points out, "coming to realize what one already knows is not readily seen
as the result of a decision."[37] It is better seen as having to do with attending
and concentrating, a shift in perspective rather than a deliberate (inten-

tional) decision. The details of this account, which turns on a nonvolitional interpretation of willing, are worked out in her recent book.[38]

Ferreira suggests that, for Kierkegaard, the act of choosing is understood primarily as an imaginative exercise through which the individual arrives at a radically new understanding of self and world. In particular, it is suggested that this imaginative transformation is effected in a manner similar to a gestalt shift.[39] The work of Thomas Kuhn provides an apt illustration of this point. In *The Structure of Scientific Revolutions,* he maintains that the transition between incommensurable scientific paradigms involves

> a reconstruction of the field from new fundamentals, a reconstruction that changes some of the field's most elementary theoretical generalizations as well as many of its paradigm methods and applications. . . . When the transition is complete, the profession will have changed its view of the field, its methods, and its goals.[40]

This kind of transition cannot be made a step at a time. "Like the gestalt shift, it must occur all at once (though not necessarily in an instant) or not at all."[41] In a similar fashion, Ferreira suggests that religious conversion occurs in a subject when a critical threshold is reached.[42] Conversion is said to consist in a new way of seeing, a new vision. Understood in terms of a gestalt shift, the actual moment of conversion does not involve a deliberate decision but is rather a spontaneous event. Seeing the emergence of a new figure in the picture is more properly described as an act of recognition than as the direct result of a decision. Although our seeing can be the indirect result of a deliberate decision to look for another pattern, the recognition itself is not the direct result of a volition. We can make ourselves look but we cannot make ourselves see (121).

That the imagination plays a crucial role in Kierkegaard's account of religious conversion is supported by his description of faith as a kind of passion. On Ferreira's view, passion qualifies the leap of faith by illuminating the role of "imaginative engagement" in the transition (114–115). This point is illustrated by analogy with the passion of love. Ferreira argues that love is constituted by a nonvolitional form of engagement, which is not the result of a deliberate decision but of a surrender of oneself to the other that is followed by a conscious affirmation (117). In contrast to traditional accounts, which posit a dichotomy between leaping and falling, Ferreira argues that love is neither purely passive nor purely active (119). It is the same with the passion of faith: "That Kierkegaard speaks of faith as both passion and leap is an indication of the mutually correcting character of the concepts–that the spontaneous, non-deliberate surrender is nevertheless active and free" (123–124). What this suggests to Ferreira is that Kierkegaard does not see the leap of faith as an act of sheer will-power, but rather as a metaphorical and imaginative process of self-reflection, which itself constitutes a change.

For the Christian, this transformation is effected in the encounter with the paradox of the God-man. The alternative to rejecting this paradox is not merely a deliberate decision to believe. Rather, faith involves the imaginative activity of holding apparently contradictory elements together. It is precisely in this state of tension, where the individual is simultaneously placed between two perspectives, that the conceptual shift takes place. To embrace the paradox of the God-man is therefore to embrace a new self-understanding and a new way of looking at the world. As Ferreira puts it, conversion is "the achievement of a clear vision which itself transforms" (66). This is not to say that there is no room for conscious decision in faith. We can, for instance, make a deliberate decision to bring about the situation where such a conceptual shift can occur; and we must at any rate make conscious decisions about whether or not we will affirm our nondeliberate commitments. The salient point, however, is that the actual moment of conversion "is not a volition, but rather a shift in perspective, an engagement or surrender, which is the achievement of imagination" (125).

Ferreira further points out that the concepts of interest and will are so intimately connected in Kierkegaard's account of subjectivity that they are virtually interchangeable. She interprets willing as a form of "interested" appropriation (126). To construe the will this way is to say that "its activity is one of *affirmation or active recognition* rather than a selection through 'will-power' from what are perceived as equally real alternatives" (127). Willing is not merely "the faculty of bringing about what does not yet exist–a causal faculty of bringing objects into existence–but rather willing is seen in terms of wanting, affirming, loving something that already exists" (129). The very possibility of transforming the old self into the new already presupposes the existence of the new self (59-60). Thus, in opposition to the accepted interpretation, which posits a radical discontinuity in the leap, Ferreira suggests that there is an underlying continuity between the Socratic form of subjectivity and Christian faith.

Ferreira makes several good points. Most important, she recognizes the need for a mediating position between volitionalist and antivolitionalist interpretations of the transition to faith. She also recognizes the element of passion in faith, and correctly notes the analogy between faith and love. What this analysis shows is that the phenomenon of personal conversion may result from a complex series of decisions, which culminate in a non-deliberate shift of perspective, a new way of seeing the world. As a description of how we come to faith, this analysis rejects the traditional dichotomy between leaping and falling in favor of an account that incorporates both active and passive elements, and stresses the centrality of imaginative activity.

One might initially object to this account on the grounds that the transition to Christian faith involves more than a mere conceptual or imaginative shift; it involves an ontological change in the subject.[43] In conversion, Kierkegaard explains, the believer "does not recollect what he is but becomes what he was not."[44] At the very least this raises a question about whether a change in the way one sees oneself and the world qualifies as a change in what one is. This is a relevant question because we are repeatedly warned in the Climacus writings against the temptation to 'naturalize' faith.[45] That is, it must not be assumed that "to be a Christian and to be a human being are identical."[46] This is not to deny that a sudden shift in perception could count as a qualitative change. After all, a transformation in one's conception of self arguably involves a qualitative alteration of consciousness, and the awakening of sin-consciousness in the individual would seem to constitute just such a change. In so far as the individual did not possess that consciousness before, and could not have brought it about by his own efforts, we could say that a qualitative change has taken place. But we need to be clear about the conditions under which that transformation is effected.

In the previous chapter we noted the distinction between the moment of incarnation and the moment of faith. It was observed that these are not really two separate moments, since the appearance of God in time first becomes a reality at the moment of faith. Although one can learn about the incarnation as an event in history, the full meaning and significance of that event (that it was God) only becomes a reality for the believer. In a similar manner, Kierkegaard distinguishes between rebirth, which he describes as a transformation of the individual, and the subsequent realization of that rebirth by the believer in faith. We are told that the learner "becomes aware of the rebirth" in the moment of faith.[47] When we place this statement beside the claim that the teacher must transform (omskabe) the learner before he can begin to teach (omdanne) him,[48] it becomes clear that the necessary condition for faith is actually bestowed prior to the transition to faith.

Here a note about translation is in order. Both *omskabe* and *omdanne* mean "to transform." The former, which Swenson quite literally and correctly renders as "recreate," refers to a kind of change that may be instantaneous. The latter, which also means "to convert," refers to a kind of change that must be effected through a gradual process of training or education. Kierkegaard's use of both terms suggests that we must distinguish between two stages of religious conversion. First, the individual undergoes a qualitative change in so far as he is made cognizant of sin. But this is not identical with conversion, nor can the individual be said to have faith in virtue of this qualitative change. It is only when the individual has thought through the implications of sin in a decisive way, when sin has acquired a decisive significance for his self-understanding, that conversion takes place and he becomes aware of the rebirth. The qualitative change that is brought about by the consciousness of sin is only realized in the individual's decision to recognize his need for redemption and to commit himself to following Christ.

Conversion occurs precisely when the individual, by assimilating the consciousness of sin, "takes leave of his former state."[49] Kierkegaard calls that former state "untruth." The transition to faith marks the movement away from untruth and toward truth. As the discussion in the *Postscript* makes clear, faith is to be understood not in terms of an instantaneous and irrevocable transformation, but as a process of appropriating the truth (imitating Christ's pattern). This process is an ethical-religious striving through which the individual becomes conformed to the mind of Christ. Since Kierkegaard tells us that the qualitative change occurs in the transition from unbelief to belief,[50] we may infer that although the learner is ontologically changed by receiving the condition, it is only when he makes the decision to follow Christ, to make Christ his teacher, that he becomes aware of his rebirth.

Because the discussion in the *Fragments* is highly condensed, it easily gives the impression that conversion is an instantaneous and irrevocable change in the individual (that the change which occurs as a result of being given the condition is itself the transition to faith). But closer examination reveals that there is a further transformation, which is signalled by the decision to accept Christ as savior. Though one's eyes are opened to sin, it is only in the decision to follow Christ, to be transformed by his saving truth, that one can be said to have faith. The main difference between this account and Ferreira's is the emphasis it places on the role of conscious decision in the transition to faith.

For Ferreira, the decision to believe is said to consist in a perspectival shift that results in a radically new way of seeing. The success of this part of the argument rests on the claim that believing is a kind of seeing. In particular, it is assumed that religious beliefs are acquired indirectly through a process of refocusing our attention on certain features of our experience. But even if we agree that believing is ordinarily something that happens to a person rather than something a person does, there may still be propositions that a person either can or should will to believe. Kierkegaard's description of the decision to believe in the truth of Christian revelation, and more specifically in the paradox of the incarnation, appears to require just such a deliberate effort. In the *Postscript,* for example, the transition to faith is said to occur in that moment at which, "with truth confronting the individual as a paradox, gripped in the anguish and pain of sin, facing the tremendous risk of the objective [uncertainty], the individual believes."[51]

Though it cannot be denied that imagination plays a role in religious conversion, we must not underestimate Kierkegaard's emphasis on the importance of conscious decision. In the *Postscript,* he explicitly describes the leap of faith as the "category of decision."[52] Indeed, the qualitative transition to faith is said to be brought about by no less than an "absolute decision."[53] As Kierkegaard puts it: "Even the longest of introductions cannot bring the individual a single step nearer to an absolute decision. For if it could, the decision would not be absolute, would not be a qualitative leap, and the individual would be deceived instead of helped."[54]

Kierkegaard's emphasis on decision in the transition to faith suggests a model of Christian conversion that differs from the one proposed by Ferreira. Such a model is developed in a recent study by Robert C. Solomon that stresses the voluntary nature of the decision to love.[55] Though Ferreira specifically criticizes Solomon's analysis in her book, a brief reconsideration of his position and Ferreira's criticisms may help to clarify an alternative interpretation of the transition to Kierkegaardian faith.

BELIEF AND THE WILL

According to Solomon, love is not merely an affirmation or a sudden recognition that one needs another person; rather it requires a fully conscious and deliberate decision (x). Recalling a personal experience, Solomon writes: "I remember rehearsing five possible consequences and conversations, weighing the not inconsiderable risks and then *leaping,* not falling, into that vast indeterminacy" (xi). Whatever else may have been there, "the love itself was a decision, a choice, a leap" (xi).

Solomon's discussion brings out the performative aspect of the love-relationship. The act of professing one's love is "not a description or a confession of feelings already felt but the creation of an *emotion*" (xi). In that very moment the word is uttered, a new relationship is created (xii). But having thus affirmed the voluntary nature of love, Solomon adds the following qualification: "To say that love is a decision . . . does *not* mean that, with a snap of the fingers, one decides to love, as one might jump off a bridge" (216). Meaningful human relationships are not created out of thin air. They may involve a great many decisions along the way, including the decision "to foster a set of conditions conducive to love" (223). Certainly, there is often much preparation that precedes the actual leap (218). But this qualification "does not prove that one cannot decide to love, only that one cannot *simply* decide to love" (218).

In his earlier book, Solomon describes love as "a new way of looking at the world."[56] For Ferreira, this admission is crucial.[57] For

> what we do in *looking for* a new way of looking at the world may well be different from what we do when we come to see it newly. Looking *for* something is a "product of will" in a different sense than is coming to see something in a new way.[58]

There is a difference between deciding to see a person differently (as more than a friend), and deciding to do those things which create the circumstances under which we might come to see that person differently. In the case of faith, there is a similar difference between deciding to believe and deciding to do those things (such as taking holy water and having masses said) which create the circumstances under which we might come to see the world with the eyes of faith. Although we can consciously decide to take steps to change the way we see ourselves and the world, we cannot simply will to see things in a different way.

However, Solomon does not attempt to identify the decision to love with the event of seeing the world in a different way (though the latter is certainly part of what it means to love). The important question raised by his account is whether there is room for intentional decision in the process of transition. The view he puts forward assumes that there is. In particular, he contends that there is a point at which one must make a pivotal decision, without which the love-relationship would not be realized. Similarly, we might interpret Kierkegaard as saying that a conscious decision must be made to enter into a relationship with God in time. To see how this interpretation differs from Ferreira's, we must look more closely at how the concept of decision is handeled in her nonvolitional account of the leap of faith.

Ferreira's analysis of religious conversion is supported by crucial references to the work of William James and Samuel Taylor Coleridge on the nature of voluntary action. In his *Biographia Literaria,* Coleridge describes the physical process of leaping as an activity that involves two distinct acts: the purely voluntary act of defying gravity in order to propel oneself forward, and the partially voluntary act of yielding to gravity in order to land on the desired spot.[59] Ferreira notes that this description is reminiscent of Kierkegaard's observation that the act of walking is at the same time a kind of falling.[60] A similar phenomenon is illustrated by James in his *Principles of Psychology,* where his analysis of the simple act of getting out of bed reveals that "we more often than not get up without any struggle or decision at all. We suddenly find that we *have* got up."[61] The act of getting up is in simple cases explained not by reference to an intentional decision on the part of the agent, but rather to what James calls a "fortunate lapse of consciousness"[62] which is followed by the agent's recognition of what happened. This fits well with Ferreira's description of the transition to faith as a shift in perspective, since for James most deliberations do end in virtue of just such a shift.[63]

This position is further supported by James's definition of the will. He explains that: "*The essential achievement of the will . . . when it is most 'voluntary,' is to attend to a difficult object and hold it fast before the mind.*"[64] Accordingly, he describes the act of changing one's mind in the following terms. First, the mind consents to the presence of a certain idea, then "clings to it, affirms it, and holds it fast, in spite of the host of exciting mental images which rise in revolt against it and would expel it from the mind" (563f.). Sustained by this "resolute effort of the will," the idea grows until finally the deliberative process ends in the recognition that one now sees the matter differently. As James puts it, "when finally the original suggestion either prevails and makes the movement take place, or gets definitively quenched by its antagonists, we are said to *decide,* or to *utter our voluntary fiat* in favor of one or the other course" (528). But this activity is more of a consent or an active recognition than it is an act of will-power. As Ferreira explains:

> The decision (or decisive movement) which occurs in virtue of
> the oscillation of our attention is not subject to "will-force" in

the way in which the effort of attention preliminary to that
decision may be. We cannot will to recognize something in the
same way that we can will to focus on what may help us to recognize it.[65]

Applying this idea to the decision to believe the Christian revelation, it is
suggested that the individual is caught in a tension between two concep-
tions of self. The attention oscillates between these two perspectives for a
time, but finally recognizes that it has come to settle on the one or the
other. To the extent that we can speak of a decision here, it is not volitional.

Although James's purpose is to show that the immense majority of
decisions are made without effort, he adds that there are nevertheless
instances of decision which do seem to involve effort. In such cases, we
feel "as if we ourselves by our own wilful act inclined the beam."[66] What
distinguishes this wilful type of decision from ordinary cases is that

> in those cases the mind at the moment of deciding on the tri-
> umphant alternative dropped the other one wholly or nearly
> out of sight, whereas here both alternatives are steadily held in
> view, and in the very act of murdering the vanquishing possi-
> bility the chooser realizes how much in that instant he is mak-
> ing himself lose. (534)

This seems like a promising way to think about the Kierkegaardian leap,
since it makes better sense of the kind of decision that faith requires.

We begin by noting that the type of decision implied by Kierkegaard's description of the leap of faith is different from those ordinary
cases of decision that, as James and Ferreira point out, do not seem to
involve any effort. Consider the following description of religious actions
which we find in the *Postscript:*

> That there are cases, particularly in connection with evil
> actions, where the transition from thought to action is scarcely
> noticeable, is not denied; but these cases have a special expla-
> nation. They show what happens when the individual is in the
> power of a habit, that through often having made the transition
> from thought to action he has lost the power to keep this tran-
> sition under the control of will. . . . That the real action often
> tends to be confused with all sorts of notions, intentions,

approximations to a decision, and so forth, and that it is seldom that anyone really acts, is not denied. On the contrary, it is assumed that just this state of affairs has contributed to the confusion with which we are here dealing. But let us take an act *sensu eminenti,* where everything stands out quite clearly. The external element in Luther's action consists in his appearance before the Diet of Worms; but from the moment that he had committed himself with entire subjective passion to his decision, so that every mere relationship of possibility to this action was interpreted by him as a temptation—from that moment he had acted.[67]

Similarly, the decision to become a Christian is an act *sensu eminenti.* Confronted by the irreducible paradox of the God-man, the individual is constantly aware of how much he risks losing. We have already noted that the believer must overcome the threat of objective uncertainty. But, as Kierkegaard tells us, this difficulty is always present in the life of faith: "If I wish to preserve myself in faith I must constantly be intent upon holding fast the objective uncertainty, so as to remain out upon the deep, over seventy thousand fathoms of water . . ."[68]

The tension that is created by the absolute paradox cannot therefore be resolved by "a fortunate lapse of consciousness." For if we look more closely at Kierkegaard's description of the leap of faith, it will be seen that it differs from Coleridge's description of leaping in one crucial respect: the idea of yielding or resting is absent from it. In the very same journal entry in which Kierkegaard describes walking as a kind of falling, he indicates the open-ended nature of the leap by observing that the objective is neither to land on the spot, nor beyond it.[69] The leap of faith must never be understood as a completed act. The decision to believe is not made once and for all; the believer is always in the process of reaffirming (preserving) his faith, always in the process of becoming a Christian. This tells us two things about the nature of that decision: first, that it requires a deliberate effort, in so far as one must accept Christ as savior and affirm one's faith in him despite the objective uncertainty of revelation; and second, that one's faith must be continually renewed. Kierkegaard sometimes expresses this latter point by saying that existence is the period of decision.[70]

God's revelation of human sinfulness makes it possible for the learner to become aware that he is in error and in need of salvation. However, this new seeing is neither identical with faith nor sufficient for conversion. The decisive transformation, which marks the transition to faith, begins with a free act of will in which the learner accepts the truth of revelation, embraces Christ as his savior, and commits himself to a life of striving to imitate the ideal pattern. This leap of faith, which can only follow from the decisive recognition that "Christ is everything" to him,[71] marks the beginning of a lifelong task. For what it means to be a Christian is that the learner is always in the process of becoming a Christian, always striving to preserve himself in faith (albeit with the aid of divine grace). The task of appropriating Christ's saving truth, as Kierkegaard describes it in the *Postscript*, requires that one hold fast to the objective uncertainty, fully aware of the risk involved. This is reflected in the definition of truth as an "*objective uncertainty held fast in an appropriation process of the most passionate inwardness.*"[72] The decision to follow Christ must be sustained by a continual effort of will.

In conclusion, it has been shown that the acquisition of faith, though a gift, requires free and active human agency. The initiative comes from God: it is only by virtue of the uncovenanted revelation of the truth about human sinfulness that divine forgiveness and reconciliation are made possible. Indeed, according to Kierkegaard, all our actions in this direction are conditioned by divine grace. However, once the truth of revelation is given, and the individual is qualified by the new consciousness of his condition, the outcome will depend in part on how the individual chooses to respond. As Kierkegaard puts it, "God can give help for what only freedom can do."[73]

Ferreira has suggested that the moment of choice is really one of coming to see that we have already decided; that we have already become engaged with a possibility in a decisive way. In her interpretation, the decision to believe is the realization of our decisive engagement with Christ. There is certainly some textual warrant for reading Kierkegaard this way. But Kierkegaard's description of the leap as involving the decision to follow Christ suggests a more pivotal role for conscious choice in effecting the transition to the faith-relationship. In this account, the learner is transformed by receiving the condition for faith, which in turn empowers him to move toward Christ. But this is not yet faith. For even though one's eyes have in this way been opened to the truth about human sinfulness and the need for redemption, the transition to faith is marked by the conscious decision to be related to Christ's saving truth through an appropriation process of the most passionate inwardness, ever mindful of the objective uncertainties attending the idea of a divine truth historically revealed.

In the following chapter, I shall examine Kierkegaard's claim that truth is subjectivity, and show how this shapes his understanding of the role of doctrine in the life of faith.

6

❧❦

Subjectivity, Truth, and Doctrine

Though Kierkegaard never explicitly formulated a theory of religious doctrine, he did have a clear position on the role that Christian doctrine ought to play in the lives of believers. Briefly stated, he maintained that Christianity, as a human activity, involves more than merely believing certain propositions about matters of fact. The doctrines of Christianity take on true religious significance only when they are given the power to transform the lives of those who accept them; only when they are given expression in the life of the believer. This was, however, far from evident to many of Kierkegaard's theological contemporaries who, under the influence of Hegelian philosophy, sought to replace the Christian virtue of faith with the philosophical ideal of objective knowledge.

To draw attention to this fact, Kierkegaard distinguished between an objective and a subjective relationship to doctrine, and stressed the centrality of the latter to the Christian life of faith. To be subjectively related to a doctrine is to see how the acceptance of it imposes certain requirements on the way one speaks and acts. By thus emphasizing the practical and ethical implications of doctrinal adherence, Kierkegaard sought to preserve the properly dogmatic content of Christianity, while rejecting that form of orthodoxy that takes intellectual assent to be the primary act of faith.

That Kierkegaard was concerned to argue for the essentially subjective character of Christian faith and truth will come as no surprise to students of the literature. What may be surprising, however, is the theory of doctrine this position seems to suggest. For in contrast to what may be called a "propositional" theory of doctrine, which says that doctrines function chiefly as informative statements or truth claims about objective realities, Kierkegaard seems to have regarded doctrines primarily as rules for regulating the speech and action of the religious community. In this latter respect, Kierkegaard's view is strikingly similar to the 'regulative' theory of doctrine recently proposed by George Lindbeck in his book *The Nature of Doctrine*.[1] According to Lindbeck, doctrines should be construed primarily as "rules of discourse, attitude, and action" (18). Although doctrinal statements can function in the manner of discursive propositions, their main function is to regulate the life of the religious community; indeed, this is the only proper function doctrines have as church teachings. The aim of the present chapter is to examine this point of similarity between Kierkegaard and the postliberal approach to the nature of religious doctrine.

THE REGULATIVE THEORY OF DOCTRINE

The regulative theory of doctrine presupposes a more general theory about the nature of religion. According to that theory, which Lindbeck characterizes as the 'cultural-linguistic' approach, religion is not pictured in a purely cognitivist manner as involving the decision to believe a proposition or follow a directive. To become religious is to interiorize a set of skills by practice and training. It is to learn how to feel, to act, and to think in conformity with a religious tradition, whose conventions are "far richer and more subtle than can be explicitly articulated" (35). Religion is here likened to a Wittgensteinian language-game, in which there are specific rules for making legitimate moves in the game—both linguistically and in the larger behavioral sense. The role assigned to doctrine is, in this approach, much like that of a grammar. As Lindbeck writes:

> Some doctrines, such as those delimiting the canon and speci-
> fying the relation of Scripture and tradition, help determine the
> vocabulary; while others (or sometimes the same ones) instan-
> tiate syntactical rules that guide the use of this material in con-
> struing the world, community, and self; and still others provide
> semantic reference. The doctrine that Jesus is the Messiah, for
> example, functions lexically as the warrant for adding the New
> Testament literature to the canon, syntactically as a hermeneu-
> tical rule that Jesus Christ be interpreted as the fulfillment of
> the Old Testament promises (and the Old Testament as point-

ing toward him), and semantically as a rule regarding the referring use of such titles as "Messiah." (81)

The analogy between doctrine and grammar reveals a good deal about the religious form of life. One point the analogy brings out is that there are two distinct ways of being related to doctrine. For just as there is a difference between knowing the rules of English grammar and being an English speaker, so is there also a difference between knowing the doctrines of Christianity and being Christian.

Learning the doctrines of Christianity, like learning the grammar of English, ordinarily (though not always) requires the memorization of official rules. But as one acquires proficiency in English, one does not continue to articulate the rules of its grammar; one rather exhibits conformity with those rules in correct patterns of speaking and writing. Similarly, in the exercise of authentic faith the life of the believer exhibits conformity with doctrine through correct patterns of speaking and acting. In this way, doctrine becomes interiorized by the believer, embedded in the religious practice.

The analogy with grammar reveals another important feature of doctrine. As far as faith is concerned, the learning of doctrine is not to be construed as an end in itself, but rather as a means of facilitating the religious form of life. True faith is exhibited primarily in correct performance, rather than in correct belief. For the religious believer, the main objective is therefore not to acquire knowledge about the religion, nor about what the religion teaches, but rather how to be religious in the ways prescribed by its doctrines (35).

In the regulative theory, doctrines do not make truth claims about objective realities, but are rather understood to regulate truth claims by excluding some and permitting others. Just as grammar by itself affirms nothing either true or false about the world in which language is used, but only about the language itself, so doctrine asserts nothing either true or false about God and his relationship to human beings, but only about such assertions. Doctrine is thus the framework that "makes possible the description of realities, the formulation of beliefs, and the experiencing of inner attitudes, feelings, and sentiments" (33).

Nevertheless, Christian doctrine does stand as an official statement of what is essential to Christianity. As such, it serves a normative function by determining what constitutes faithful adherence. Religious pretenders are exposed by virtue of failing to behave in accordance with specific doctrinal requirements. Those requirements, once again, cannot be satisfied merely by repeating official teachings or catechisms. Authentic religious commitment is reflected not merely in what the believer says, but in how the believer's words are interwoven with relevant patterns of thought and action.

Although the primary function of Christian doctrine is, in this formulation, to regulate the Christian way of life, it is necessary to address the question of its ontological truth. For when Christians proclaim the doctrine of revelation, they typically mean to assert that the narrative of Christ's life, teaching, death, and resurrection is an objectively true account of those events. But can the regulative theory, which emphasizes the cultural and linguistic features of Christianity, account for this cognitive dimension of faith?

This seems doubtful, at least within the philosophical tradition that ties meaning and truth to individual statements. But it is just this tradition that Lindbeck disputes (64–68). The standard cognitivist view is that statements refer to objective realities by means of linguistic conventions that specify an appropriate correspondence relation between statements and their referents. In opposition to this view, Lindbeck contends that meaning and truth are not simply a function of individual statements exhibiting a neutral correspondence relation to facts about the world. Our statements do not confront the world individually, but as a system; that is, through the way they function in a particular conceptual scheme and its peculiar syntax. As one commentator has observed, sentences such as 'God is three persons in one' are not to be construed as referring to some discrete fact about the deity in the same way that 'three persons are here' refers to a state of affairs in the world. The entire system of Christian doctrine in which trinitarian language plays a role must be taken into account in order to make sense of this unique reference.[2] There is therefore a sense in which those who are unskilled in the language of Christianity, those who are unacquainted with its doctrines, not only cannot affirm assertions of religious beliefs, but cannot deny these either.[3]

According to Lindbeck's coherence-based theory, sentences acquire enough referential specificity to admit of truth or falsity only within the context of a determinate conceptual system. In the case of religious language, this specificity is supplied by the religious context: the form of life in which it occurs and the doctrines that regulate its use. In this view, a religious statement will be judged true if it fits into the total pattern of speech and action; false if it is inconsistent with what the pattern as a whole affirms. At this level, a statement such as 'Jesus is the Messiah' will be true, provided that its use is consistent with the form of life prescribed by the biblical stories.

However, ontological truth does require more than mere coherence among the statements that comprise a system of religious belief. For coherence alone does not establish an appropriate correspondence between religious statements and their referents. According to Lindbeck, religious statements are unique in that the correspondence they bear to reality is a function of the way they shape a form of life, which itself corresponds to divine reality (68). This is similar to what J. L. Austin has called the "performatory" use of language.[4] From this perspective, a religious statement acquires the status of an ontological truth only in so far as it is a performance that creates a correspondence between self and God. In this comprehensive sense of correspondence, truth is characterized as the relation between a way of living in the world and the will of God. The correspondence religious statements bear to reality is "not an attribute that they have when considered in and of themselves, but is only a function of their role in constituting a form of life ... which itself corresponds to the Most Important, the Ultimately Real."[5]

According to Lindbeck, this 'performative-propositionalism' is consistent with the modest form of cognitivism advocated by Aquinas:

> Aquinas holds that although in statements about God the human mode of signifying (*modus significandi*) does not correspond to anything in the divine being, the signified (*significatum*) does. Thus, for example, when we say that God is good, we do not affirm that any of our concepts of goodness (*modi significandi*) apply to him, but rather that there is a concept of goodness unavailable to us, viz., God's understanding of his own goodness, which does apply. What we assert, in other words, is that "'God is good' is meaningful and true," but without knowing the meaning of "God is good." (66)

The salient point of this discussion is to show that it is not the primary aim of doctrine to provide falsifiable descriptions of historical events. We do not really know, for example, how the biblical story of Christ's resurrection signifies. The only way to assert the truth of this central doctrine is to do something about it, to commit oneself passionately to thinking and acting in the belief that the resurrection did in fact take place. In effect, Lindbeck is concerned to argue that the only way to assert the truth of the resurrection is to "commit oneself to a way of life; and this concern is wholly congruent with the suggestion that it is only through the performatory use of religious statements that they acquire propositional force" (66).

What the 'cognitive-propositional' account of religion fails to see is that a religious system "is more like a natural language than a formally organized set of explicit statements, and that the right use of this language . . . cannot be detached from a particular way of behaving" (64). This same point is made by Wittgenstein, who argues that the religious believer who understands himself in his faith does not use the language of hypothesis or opinion, knowledge or probability.[6] His belief is grounded rather in a form of life, in the way his life is regulated by a doctrine (54).

According to Wittgenstein, the Christian belief in a final judgment is not simply a matter of thinking it highly probable that some future event will take place. Here, religious belief is more like having a picture and a technique for using it (56). For the believer, the picture of a final judgment is constantly in the foreground, regulating his life, whereas for those who do not believe, such a picture simply has no use; they think differently, live differently.[7]

We might say that doctrine tells us what the picture is and specifies the proper techniques for using it. In other words, doctrine tells us how certain pictures are to regulate our lives by specifying the various ways in which they govern the attitudes and actions of believers.[8] "Rules of life," says Wittgenstein, "are dressed up in pictures. And these pictures can only serve to *describe* what we are to do, not *justify* it."[9] According to Lindbeck, the reasonableness of a religious picture is a function of its ability to provide an intelligible interpretation of the believer's experiences. Christianity is a comprehensive "cultural-linguistic" system that "shapes the entirety of life and thought."[10]

This shaping power reaches the concepts, experiences, and beliefs to which we appeal in the justification of various religious statements and actions. As a result, religions cannot be demonstrated or refuted, since "theoretical frameworks shape perceptions of problems and their possible solutions in such a way that each framework is in itself irrefutable" (33). However, as Lindbeck notes, religious belief systems are subject to a kind of rational testing procedure similar to that which applies to scientific paradigms, where confirmation or disconfirmation depends on how successful they are in making practical and coherent sense of human experience (131). Various doctrinal formulations are abandoned, not so much because they are refuted on their own terms, but because they prove unfruitful in the light of new or different questions that challenge the community of believers (42).

When propositionally construed, doctrines encourage us to focus on the rationality or soundness of religious belief. But as Wittgenstein has observed, sound doctrines are really useless for religious purposes.[11] For doctrines must be interiorized through acts of obedience and worship; they must become integrated in a form of life. And this is precisely where the passion comes in:

> It strikes me that a religious belief could only be something like a passionate commitment to a system of reference. Hence, although it's *belief*, it's really a way of living, or a way of assessing life. It's passionately seizing hold of *this* interpretation. Instruction in a religious faith, therefore, would have to take the form of a portrayal, a description, of that system of reference, while at the same time being an appeal to conscience. And this combination would have to result in the pupil himself, of his own accord, passionately taking hold of the system of reference. (64e)

Religious belief, according to Lindbeck and Wittgenstein, has to do above all with existence, with changing the direction of one's life (53e). For them, genuine faith is not merely a doctrine or a proposition, but a passion that takes hold of one; a passion that is exhibited in the commitment to live for an ideal. For the Christian believer, the form of this life is 'regulated' in all its aspects by reference to the life, teaching, death, and resurrection of Jesus Christ as that is depicted in the doctrinal narratives of the New Testament.[12] In the following section, I shall attempt to show that the salient features of this regulative theory of doctrine are anticipated in Kierkegaard's analysis of subjectivity and religious truth.

KIERKEGAARD ON SUBJECTIVITY AND RELIGIOUS TRUTH

I want to begin by suggesting that Kierkegaard's celebrated distinction between objectivity and subjectivity may properly be understood as designating two ways of being related to Christian doctrine. The distinction is intended to draw attention to the difference between merely knowing what Christianity is and being Christian. In the *Postscript*, Kierkegaard says it is possible to "consider objectively what Christianity is in that the inquirer sets the question objectively before him, leaving aside for the present the question of its truth (the truth is subjectivity)."[13] It is thus directly affirmed by Johannes Climacus that one can know what Christianity is without being a Christian.[14]

This distinction is an important one for Kierkegaard, whose avowed aim in the *Postscript* is to elucidate the true requirements for personal salvation. Because salvation is predicated on the relationship one bears to Christian doctrine, Kierkegaard begins by asking what the proper relationship to that doctrine must be.[15] It is explained that the objective relationship to doctrine is an intellectual one.[16] The objective inquirer merely raises the question of the truth of Christianity and assumes that an answer can be arrived at either by historical or philosophical inquiry. But Kierkegaard contends that neither of these objective modes of inquiry can yield knowledge of the truth of Christianity. Let us review these arguments briefly.

The historical inquiry takes the Scriptures as its objective point of reference.[17] There are two main forms this inquiry can take. The first is purely philological in scope and seeks to render the biblical text in its most accurate form. Such a task is, in Kierkegaard's view, perfectly legitimate and meaningful.[18] The second form of inquiry, which comes under the heading "critical theology," differs from that of philology in one important respect. Though both regard the task of textual criticism as central to the theological enterprise, critical theology seeks to draw the further conclusion that the believer can base his salvation on these writings.[19] However, according to Kierkegaard, historical inquiry proves wholly inadequate as a basis for salvation:

> When Christianity is viewed from the standpoint of its historical documentation, it becomes necessary to secure an entirely trustworthy account of what the Christian doctrine is. If the inquirer were infinitely interested in behalf of his relationship to the doctrine he would at once despair; for nothing is more readily evident than that the greatest attainable certainty with respect to anything historical is merely an *approximation*. And an approximation, when viewed as a basis for an eternal happiness, is wholly inadequate, since the incommensurability makes a result impossible.[20]

Kierkegaard's point about the incommensurability between faith and historical inquiry is supported by the following argument. Suppose that historical inquiry establishes the canonicity of the books of the Bible, that their reports are shown to be perfectly authentic. Has anyone who did not previously have faith been brought any closer to faith? Kierkegaard answers in the negative: "Faith does not simply result from a scientific inquiry; it does not come directly at all. On the contrary, in this objective inquiry one tends to lose that infinite personal interestedness in passion which is the condition of faith."[21]

Suppose now that the situation is reversed: the antagonists of faith succeed in making their case against the Scriptures on the grounds that the sources are shown to be unreliable, even contradictory. Is Christianity thereby abolished? Kierkegaard reasons that it is not:

> Because these books are not written by these authors, are not authentic, are not in an integral condition, are not inspired (though this cannot be proved, since it is an object of faith), it does not follow that these authors have not existed; and above all, it does not follow that Christ has not existed. In so far, the believer is equally free to assume it.[22]

The argument here is not that the Scriptures should not be accepted as true, but that the significance of religious conviction does not depend on a truth value.

The truth of Christianity is not a historical truth, but a spiritual one. Truth, in the sense in which Christianity is the truth, is not "an immediate and extremely free-and-easy relationship between an immediate consciousness and a sum of propositions."[23] Spiritual truth does not manifest itself in the individual's objective acceptance of a doctrine, but rather in the mode of the individual's relationship to that doctrine. It is only to the extent that one strives to be subjectively related to Christian doctrine, to give it existential expression, that one can be said to be "in the truth."[24]

In Kierkegaard's view, even if one could attain empirical certainty regarding the authenticity of the Scriptures, the task of acquiring and preserving faith would not be helped by this. The sort of certainty that derives from historical or scientific inquiry is not even desirable, since the objective form of belief which results from such inquiries is neither a necessary nor a sufficient basis for faith. In line with the regulative view, Kierkegaard affirms that faith is primarily a matter of correct performance as opposed to correct belief.

The main failure of the speculative view as it relates to doctrine can now be stated briefly as follows. The speculative inquirer treats doctrine as a body of philosophical statements that are to be explained and understood on purely intellectual terms. He assumes that knowledge is higher than faith, or the key to a more profound expression of faith. The result, in either case, is the reduction of Christianity to mere "doctrinal propositions," and the reduction of Christian faith to an act of intellectual assent.[25]

On the one hand, the speculative approach leaves out of account the existential requirements of doctrinal acceptance:

> Surely it is one thing for something to be a philosophical doctrine which desires to be intellectually grasped and speculatively understood, and quite another thing to be a doctrine that proposes to be realized in existence. . . . Christianity is a doctrine of this kind. To speculate upon it is a misunderstanding, and the farther one goes in this direction the greater is the misunderstanding.[26]

On the other hand, the speculative philosopher claims to be able to explain or understand that which proclaims itself a paradox.[27] As I read Kierkegaard, the paradoxical quality of Christianity lies in the fact that it is revealed in history, and yet its content is such that it transcends all historical categories of understanding. It does not follow from this, however, that Christianity is nonsense. Kierkegaard agrees with Pascal that God is incomprehensible to the human intellect. God's revelation in history is not paradoxical from the standpoint of eternity, but only in relation to a finite human being, whose intellect is limited by historical categories.[28]

Christianity therefore rejects every attempt to treat it as an ordinary historical event. Properly understood, the narrative of Christian revelation does not present itself as an object for historical belief; it is not intended to be understood as a falsifiable description of a historical event. Rather, it presents a radically new conceptual framework for understanding self and world. Religious belief is more like a conviction, a passionate commitment to the form of life depicted in the biblical narratives.

Here again, Wittgenstein's perspective is illuminating. In a passage that seems clearly to be inspired by a reading of Kierkegaard, he writes:

> Christianity is not based on a historical truth; rather, it offers us a (historical) narrative and says: now believe! But not, believe this narrative with the belief appropriate to a historical narrative; rather: believe through thick and thin, which you can do only as the result of a life. *Here you have a narrative, don't take the same attitude to it as you take to other historical narratives!* Make a

quite different place in your life for it.–There is nothing *paradoxical* about that![29]

The word *belief* as it is used here by Wittgenstein, and by Kierkegaard in many places,[30] does not describe a propositional attitude toward an ordinary historical event. Christianity does not rest on a historical basis in the sense that ordinary belief in historical facts could serve as a foundation.[31] This is precisely the point that Kierkegaard makes when he says that the attempt to safeguard faith by means of an objective inquiry confuses the object of faith with a simple historical fact.[32]

If Christianity were merely an event of historical interest, then it would indeed be appropriate to treat it on a par with other historical facts. However, it has already been noted that Christianity does not present itself as an object for historical knowledge, but as an occasion for spiritual transformation. According to Kierkegaard, the only relationship an existing individual can have to Christ is a spiritual one, whereby the individual strives to shape his life in conformity with the ideal pattern.[33] Therefore truth is not based on the traditional picture of correspondence between mind and reality, but between self and God.

For Kierkegaard, Christ represents the ideal embodiment of the doctrine (the Word revealed in flesh). He *is* the truth, and the task of faith is to reduplicate his pattern in such a way that one's own life becomes an expression of the truth.[34] This is a doctrine to be followed rather than interpreted; its primary purpose is to describe what I, as a Christian, am to do. To regard Christianity as merely a 'sum of doctrinal propositions' is to turn it into something essentially different; it is to miss the whole point of the existential communication.

It is repeatedly asserted throughout the authorship that the only way to be related to the truth of Christianity is through the subjectivity of faith.[35] I have suggested that this is the condition of the individual who wills to conform his life to Christ's. Nevertheless, there is manifested in this subjective relationship to doctrine a kind of objectivity. As Kierkegaard notes:

> In all that is usually said about Johannes Climacus being purely subjective . . . people have forgotten . . . that in one of the final sections he shows that the remarkable thing is that there is a "how" which has the property that when it is present the "what" is also present; and this is the "how" of "faith."[36]

Some commentators have taken this as evidence that Kierkegaard thought there could be objective knowledge of the truth of Christianity.[37] However, it is unlikely that Kierkegaard intended by this remark to give objectivity any priority in matters of faith, since he already stated that objectivity, when it ranks as highest, is precisely irreligious.[38] A better clue to interpreting Kierkegaard's meaning is contained in the following passage from *Practice in Christianity*, where it is explained that

> when one is the truth and when the requirement is to be truth, to know the truth is an untruth. For knowing the truth is something that entirely of itself accompanies being the truth, not the other way around. . . . Indeed, one cannot really know the truth, for if one knows the truth one must, of course, know that the truth is to be the truth, and then in one's knowledge of the truth one would know that to know truth is an untruth.[39]

The distinction drawn here is between knowing the truth in the sense that one knows what the Christian doctrine is, and knowing the truth in the sense that to know the truth is to be the truth. Thus, as I understand this passage, to be Christian in the proper ways does involve a knowledge of what Christianity is. The subjectivity wherein religious truth lies is regulated by reference to an objective body of doctrines. In this manner, the objective 'what' of Christianity can truly be said to be given in the subjective 'how' of faith, in so far as the doctrine is given expression in the life of the believer.

To be a Christian, for Kierkegaard, means no less than to enter into a form of life that is regulated in all its aspects by the biblical stories depicting Christ's life, teaching, death, and resurrection. The narratives of the New Testament form the basis for a comprehensive doctrinal scheme, which not only structures all the dimensions of religious existence, but also serves as an objective standard for determining what constitutes faithful adherence to the Christian community.

In line with the regulative view, Kierkegaard affirms that the truth of Christianity cannot be found in the direction suggested by a propositional view of doctrine, since its emphasis on correct belief encourages the reification of doctrine and fails to account for the constitutive role of passion and action in the religious life. Rather, Kierkegaard holds that the true purpose of doctrine is to shape the subjectivity of the individual, thereby bringing the individual into conformity with the truth. For the truth, in the sense that Christianity is the truth, is a life.

But to say that the truth of Christianity is a life is not to say that religious beliefs are devoid of cognitive content. Lindbeck carefully distances himself from a noncognitivist position by affirming that the believer does take himself to be related to an independent reality. He speaks of the religious form of life, in its totality, as a proposition. There is thus affirmed a sort of correspondence between the totality of Christian thought and practice, the Christian form of life, and the ultimate reality of things. The religious form of life is a true proposition to the extent that its objectivities are interiorized in such a way as to conform the individual to the ultimate goodness and reality of things; and it is a false proposition to the extent that this conformity is not realized.[40]

The insight here is essentially Kierkegaardian. The religious value of doctrinal statements, according to Kierkegaard, lies in the fact that they are vehicles for being related to divine reality or living "in the truth." Doctrinal statements do not purport to be falsifiable descriptions of what divine reality is like, but rather specify how it is possible to participate in that reality. The truth of Christianity is not a static (eternal) relation between a statement and an objective state of affairs, but rather a relationship between an existing individual and God; a relationship, moreover, that is effected through the acquisition of a set of skills. One is not related to God by getting the so-called right description of the divine nature or by bolstering one's beliefs with rational justifications. As Kierkegaard observes, God is present only to the existing individual in faith.[41]

But even if we grant that religious truth is grounded in the correspondence between a way of living in the world and the will of God, and that faith cannot be reduced to the affirmation of doctrinal propositions, this still leaves a question concerning the justification for believing that Christian doctrine, or any other body of religious doctrine, actually directs its adherents to the truth. For this presumably depends upon whether there is any justification for believing in the independent reality of the divine.

Although Lindbeck fails to provide such a justification, there is a ready philosophical framework within which the regulative theory may be grounded. In the *Critique of Pure Reason*, Kant demonstrates that all metaphysical debates are essentially inconclusive, since transcendental reason is not equipped to deal with matters of eternal concern, and reason devoid of sense data can prove anything. But because God and immortality are necessary postulates for human life, he argues that it must be rationally permissible to predicate them as existing:

We may therefore be so completely assured that no one will ever prove the opposite, that there is no need for us to concern ourselves with formal arguments. We are always in a position to accept these propositions–propositions which are so very closely bound up with the speculative interest of our reason in its empirical employment, and which, moreover, are the sole means of reconciling the speculative with the practical interest.[42]

In chapter 3 I argued that this is essentially the same position taken by Kierkegaard. As a conceptual expression for the total incommensurability between an infinite God and a finite human intellect, the absolute paradox clears logical space for faith by showing that theoretical reason is incapable of deciding the question of whether Christianity is true. But where our theoretical reason is unable to decide the option between belief and unbelief, and an eternal happiness hangs in the balance, the venture to believe may be validated on practical grounds.

Thus, I find in Lindbeck's proposal a natural affinity to the pragmatist tradition in religious thought, a tradition represented by Pascal, Kant, Kierkegaard, and William James. Whether or not he would accept this characterization of his position, it does provide an appropriate justification for adopting the conceptual scheme of the religious life. Moreover, it is fully compatible with the larger ecumenical purposes of Lindbeck's book.[43]

WORD AND SPIRIT:
THE CRITIQUE OF CHRISTENDOM

As we have seen, it is possible to have an objective understanding of what Christian doctrine says and what the Christian form of life requires. But it is quite another thing to be subjectively related to the content of that doctrine: to interiorize it in and through religious practice. Authentic religious commitment is expressed not only in what a believer says, but in how the believer's words are interwoven with a specific pattern of thought and action. In the case of Christianity, this pattern is objectively specified with reference to the Christ-revelation.

This distinction lies at the heart of Kierkegaard's critique of modern Christendom. It is important to recognize that the object of his attack is not Christian doctrine, but rather the tendency in Christendom to view faith as a purely objective relation to that doctrine.[44] Kierkegaard believed that the state church had gradually been reduced to a symbol of bourgeois Protestant culture, so that being a Christian was confirmed by the fact that one had been born and baptized in Denmark. As one commentator puts it, Protestantism had "domesticated Christian commitment until it entailed little more than a well-upholstered family life, solid citizenship, and what is nowadays identified as the Protestant work ethic."[45] Far from taking a decisive stance in opposition to worldliness, Christianity had become fully integrated with the secular order:

> Even if one deigned to take a pew on the principal feast days, the pulpit seldom pummeled you. The consolations of religion were admirably set forth. Of its possible perturbations, little was to be heard. An ominous silence reigned. *This* is the kind of setup Kierkegaard was attacking. He took his stand not against Christianity but against 'the blinding illusion of Christendom,' the 'geographical Christianity' he so witheringly described in the *The Book on Adler*. He opposed the equation: *Mængden = Menigheden* (the crowd is identical with the congregation, the Church the same as the State, Christianity coterminous with the world).[46]

Even if the congregation consisted entirely of true disciples, this would not constitute the basis for an "established" church.[47] For the only true church, in Kierkegaard's view, is a militant church; one that acknowledges that its authority is dialectically conditioned by the transcendent revelation it has received.

Kierkegaard also discerned an intellectual threat to Christianity in the form of Hegelian speculative philosophy. It was noted earlier that speculation encourages an objective relation to doctrine by placing knowledge above faith, and by making rational comprehension the highest attainment in the realm of spirit. In sharp contrast to the Hegelian view, Kierkegaard stressed that revelation situates the individual before God, who is wholly other, and requires that the individual seek redemption through a life of ethical-religious striving in faith. He deplored the Hegelian systematization of salvation history that erases the absolute distinction between the divine and the human, and shifts the emphasis decidedly away from existence and the ethical, thereby removing what is essential to Christianity.

The seriousness of the threat posed by Christian speculation can be seen in the context of Kierkegaard's view of religious language, and the role that it plays in the development of the self. For it is only when a person recognizes and accepts responsibility for his words and actions that he can truly be said to "choose himself." In this act of subjective appropriation a person is both "revealed and constituted" as the self he is called to be.[48] Moreover, since Kierkegaard's definition of the self is at the same time a definition of what it means to be spirit, it follows that spirit is actualized only when a person fully accepts responsibility for his words and the commitments they entail.

But, as Kierkegaard points out, the language of Christianity is unlike the language of secular humanism or speculative philosophy, in so far as it commits one to a recognizably different way of thinking, speaking, and acting. Whether or not a certain attitude or emotion is properly Christian must be "checked by the definition of concepts," and when it is "transposed or expressed in words in order to be communicated, this transposition must occur constantly within the definition of the concepts."[49] To qualify as Christian, an experience must be defined within the doctrinal framework of Christianity. Consequently, if one does not have a firm grasp of Christian doctrinal concepts, then one cannot understand what it means to be a Christian, or what the life of faith requires. It is in this sense that Kierkegaard sees Christian speculation as an obstacle to the development of spirit.

The spiritlessness characteristic of Christendom is not equivalent to the mere absence of spirit, and hence, properly speaking, it must be distinguished from paganism. The difference, as Kierkegaard explains, is that while paganism represents a movement toward spirit, spiritlessness represents a movement away from spirit.[50] The irony is that only one who has become conscious of spirit in relation to the Christian revelation can be spiritless in this sense. The monstrous illusion of Christendom can therefore be expressed more precisely as a "spiritual denial of spirit."[51]

Stephen Crites is surely correct in pointing out that the object of Kierkegaard's polemic against Christendom was the idea that "bourgeois Protestantism or Hegelian 'spirit' were in any sense manifestations of genuine Christianity."[52] However, Kierkegaard's concern about the influence of Hegelianism was really much deeper than this statement suggests. For what he saw in the Hegelian interpretation of Christian concepts was a very grave threat to the possibility of regaining true Christian understanding. The great scandal of modern Christendom was that the language of Christian theological discourse had become volatilized by speculative philosophy. Orthodox doctrinal concepts had been evacuated of their true meanings, and had thus lost their power to shape the subjectivity of the

Christian believer. Only in Christendom could it be said of an ordained minister that he lacked "any sort of conception of the qualitative and specific peculiarity of Christianity."[53] Such was Kierkegaard's estimation of Adler, whose tragic fate provided a unique illustration of the religious confusion of the modern age.

In the following chapter I shall examine how Kierkegaard brings his analysis of Christian doctrinal concepts to bear in the case of Adler.

7

❧❧

Revelation and Religious Authority

Adolph Peter Adler first attracted the attention of the ecclesiastical authorities with the publication of a collection of sermons.[1] It was not the content of his sermons that gave cause for concern, however, but the preface to the volume, in which Adler asserted that a new doctrine had been revealed to him by Jesus Christ. Kierkegaard quotes the controversial passage:

> One evening I had just developed the origin of evil, when I saw, illuminated as by a flash of lightening, that everything depends, not upon thought, but upon the Spirit. That night a hateful sound went through our chamber. The Savior bade me to stand up and go in and write down the words.[2]

Adler further asserted in the preface that he was not only instructed to burn his earlier Hegelian writings and hold to the Bible, but that many of the sermons contained in the book were actually written with the "cooperative grace of Jesus."[3] Because of the heretical nature of these and other pronouncements which Adler would publish in a subsequent volume,[4] he was deemed unfit to continue in his post and suspended in January 1844 pending further inquiry. Early in the following year a series of questions were put to him by Bishop Mynster. Adler was asked whether or not he recognized that he was in "an exalted and confused state of mind" when he wrote and published his two works,[5] and whether he thought it "fanatical and wrong to expect and to follow such supposed revelations" as those described in the preface to his collection of sermons.[6] He was eventually dismissed from his post after replying in an evasive manner to these and similar questions.[7]

Having recently completed work on the *Postscript*, Kierkegaard now turned his attention to a closer examination of the case of Adler. This examination was facilitated in part by the simultaneous appearance of four new Adler books, which Kierkegaard immediately purchased.[8] He also found a large amount of useful information in Adler's earlier published account of the events that led to his dismissal.[9] It is believed that Kierkegaard probably began working on the manuscript sometime during the summer of 1846; and though a first draft was completed within months, he would continue to make substantial revisions to the text for nearly two years. For various reasons, the book itself remained unpublished during Kierkegaard's lifetime.[10] However, a portion of the text, containing no direct references to Adler, was eventually published in an essay entitled "On the Difference Between a Genius and an Apostle."[11]

In the introduction to his translation of *On Authority and Revelation*, Walter Lowrie remarks that this book is not to be reckoned among Kierkegaard's most important writings. It is my contention, however, that the book on Adler is integral to Kierkegaard's overall philosophical project of clarifying the requirements of Christian faith, and that by emphasizing the importance of the objective aspect of Christianity, it can be seen to complete the analysis begun in the Climacus writings. For as we have seen, Kierkegaard's claim that Christian faith exists only in the subjective appropriation of the truth is qualified by the further claim that the Christian form of life must be shaped by reference to dogmatic Christian concepts. Thus the danger posed by the influence of speculative philosophy is not merely that it encourages an objective relation to doctrine, but that by volatilizing the language of Christian theology it threatens to undermine the very possibility of being religious in the Christian sense. Kierkegaard's polemic against the Hegelian Adler is motivated by the belief that speculative theology is essentially anti-Christian.

THE ANTI-CHRISTIANITY OF HEGEL

The formal structure of Hegel's mature writings would seem to suggest that Christianity held a special place in his philosophy. The Christian religion is prominently discussed in the *Phenomenology of Mind*, in the *Encyclopedia of the Philosophical Sciences*, and in the *Lectures on the Philosophy of Religion*, which were delivered in Berlin between 1821 and 1831. As a revealed religion, Christianity represents for Hegel the culmination of the historical development of religious awareness. Not only does it afford the highest degree of self-consciousness possible in a religion, but the incarnation marks a crucial moment in the progressive self-realization of divine spirit. Nevertheless, Hegel's reputation as the "greatest abstract thinker of Christianity" has been challenged by more than one critic of his philosophy. For even though Christianity represents for him the highest dialectical stage of religious development, it is not yet the truth. Religion still operates at the level of metaphor and myth; its main ideas are communicated by means of unsystematized images and representations. Although these serve a purpose in helping us to comprehend the content of religion, they are inferior modes of knowing. In order to make religion intelligible, philosophy must divest it of its mythological trappings. But what is this demythologized version of Christianity? Robert C. Solomon explains:

> It is a faith without icons, images, stories and myths, without miracles, without a resurrection, without a nativity, without Chartres and Fra Angelico, without wine and wafers, without Heaven and Hell, without Go as judge and without Judgment. . . . The incarnation no longer refers to Christ alone, but only to the philosophical thesis that there is no God other than humanity.[12]

Far from defending Christianity, Hegel refashions it in the image of his own secular humanism.

Hegel does not directly attack Christian theology in any of his published writings.[13] But when the doctrines of Christianity are reinterpreted in the categories of speculative philosophy, nothing Christian remains. Thus Kierkegaard remarks in the *Postscript* that, "in relation to Christianity, speculative philosophy is merely skilled in the use of all sorts of diplomatic phraseology, which deceives the unsuspicious."[14] This threat to Christianity is really much more subtle and dangerous than any previous attacks on orthodoxy:

> The greater honesty in even the most bitter attacks of an earlier age upon Christianity was that the essentially Christian was fairly well allowed to remain intact. The danger in Hegel was that he altered Christianity—and thereby achieved agreement with his philosophy. In general it is characteristic of an age of reason not to let the task remain intact and say: No—but to alter the task and then say: Yes, of course, we are agreed. The hypocrisy of reason is infinitely treacherous. This is why it is so difficult to take aim.[15]

Kierkegaard was one of the few thinkers of his day who clearly discerned this threat to Christian orthodoxy, pointing out that the most dangerous enemy of Christianity is not the one who openly criticizes the church, but the one who appears to be sympathetic with it, while subverting its foundations from within. It is in this light that we can begin to appreciate the seriousness of Adler's religious confusion.

THE BOOK ON ADLER

In the second preface to *On Authority and Revelation*, Kierkegaard writes: "My Reader, may I simply beg you to read this book, for it is important for my main effort, wherefore I am minded to recommend it."[16] The "main effort" to which he alludes is that of making it eminently clear what is involved in becoming a Christian. Specifically, it is the effort to reintroduce Christianity into Christendom by clarifying the ethical implications of faith. The Climacus writings had already made a substantial contribution in this direction by making a fundamental distinction between objective and subjective truth. According to the analysis of Christian revelation presented in those works, there can be no objective relationship to God.[17] Even if it were possible to have objective knowledge of the truth of Christianity, the result would be inimical to the spiritual development of the self. The truth of Christianity must be existentially appropriated, that is, it must be given expression in the life of the individual who accepts it.

The focus of *On Authority and Revelation* is once again on the ethical realm. As Kierkegaard explains in the preface:

> The whole book is essentially an ethical investigation of the concept of revelation; about what it means to be called by a revelation. . . . Or, what comes to the same thing, the whole book is an investigation of the concept of authority, about the confusion involved in the fact that the concept of authority has been entirely forgotten in our confused age.[18]

In this book he sets out to show how the Christian concepts of authority and revelation are to be ethically understood. To have an ethical understanding of a concept is to see how one is required to act in relation to it. This is precisely what has been forgotten in Christendom through the volatilization of dogmatic Christian concepts. In Christendom, people continue to talk about themselves as Christians and to characterize their lives in terms of Christian concepts, though they do this without a genuine awareness of the deep contradiction between their manner of speaking and living and the ethical requirements of faith.

This book reflects Kierkegaard's belief that the age must be reeducated in dogmatic Christian concepts and reawakened to the ethical implications of their use. He wants to show that a person has no right to call himself a Christian as long as he continues to live without regard for the concerns, feelings, convictions, and obligations essential to Christian faith. By explicating and defending dogmatic concepts, Kierkegaard wants to encourage the reader to be honest with himself about how he stands in relation to Christianity. He challenges the so-called Christian of Christendom to examine whether the way he lives his life is consistent with the Christian concepts he professes. This consistency is checked against the objective standard implicit in the Christian concept of revelation. As Ronald Hustwit points out:

> This consistency is the limit of an ethical understanding of theological concepts. Under its limits one cannot mean anything one wants by these concepts. They are not just subjective in this sense. Neither can one make up their use to fit some other purpose. . . . This criterion of internal consistency in an ethical understanding demands a faithfulness to the given content of Christianity, i.e., to the theological concepts as they have been revealed.[19]

This is what Kierkegaard means when he says that "Christianity is built upon a revelation, but also it is limited by the definite revelation it has received."[20] The Christ-revelation is thus the starting point for a proper definition of Christian theological concepts. It is for this reason that Kierkegaard stresses the need to call attention to the "ideal picture of being a Christian," that is, to the life and person of Christ.[21] For the life of the teacher represents the ideal ethical-religious standard to which every Christian life is to be compared. And it is to this standard that Kierkegaard finally compares Adler's speech and conduct in judging that he has misunderstood the concepts of authority and revelation.

However, the case of Adler places the issue of faith in a new light. In the Climacus writings, Kierkegaard is principally concerned to point out the difference between the speculative and Christian positions, a difference which is brought out by reference to the concept of subjectivity. The chief complaint about speculative philosophy is that it abolishes Christianity by making it into something objective, an object for rational inquiry.[22] In the book on Adler the focus is more narrowly conceived, and the complaint is more specific. He writes not for the general public, but for theologians. As Kierkegaard explains in the first preface to the book:

> Essentially this book can be read only by theologians, and among these again it essentially can interest only the individual in so far as he, instead perhaps of becoming self-important and setting himself up as my judge . . . undertakes the labor of reading and then perceives in what sense A. is the subject of this book, and in what sense he is used to throw light upon the age and to defend dogmatic concepts, in what sense there is just as much attention paid to the age as to Adler.[23]

Having shown the qualitative difference between speculative and Christian categories, he now examines how the speculative volatilization of the language of Christian theology undermines the possibility of actualizing spirit. Adler is not held up as an example of one who is lacking in passion or inwardness, but as one whose passion is not grounded in a proper understanding of Christian concepts. Adler is so thoroughly imbued with Hegelian ideas and concepts that there is no hope that he could understand himself in relation to his claim to having a revelation. But even worse, he does not realize the disparity between his speculative understanding of Christian concepts and what they really mean. Concerning the concept of revelation, Kierkegaard points out that speculative philosophy "has not bluntly denied it, but it has volatilized it so far that at last it becomes a determinant of subjectivity, the simple identity of subject-object."[24] To address this problem, a different strategy is required. Here the stress must be placed on the objective content of Christianity. As the English title of the work suggests, Kierkegaard's analysis focuses on the concepts of authority and revelation.

ON AUTHORITY AND REVELATION

A person who is entrusted with a divine communication is thereby placed in a position of authority with respect to others. This is a derived authority, which has its ground in the authority of God. The person who is thus called by God receives a mission: "The doctrine imparted to him is not given to him as a problem to ponder over, it is not given to him for his own sake; on the contrary, he is on a mission and has to proclaim the doctrine and exercise authority."[25] It is emphasized that one who is called by a revelation is obliged to appeal to that revelation, to exert authority on the strength of having been called by God.[26] Kierkegaard is aware that the word *authority* has a variety of uses apart from the Christian context. He mentions, for example, that it has a valid application in political, social, civic, domestic, and disciplinary relationships.[27] It is crucial to notice, however, that the Christian concept of authority cannot be assimilated to any of these uses. Kierkegaard wants to call our attention to the qualitative distinctiveness of the Christian concept of authority.[28]

By claiming to have received a special revelation, Adler puts himself in the category of an apostle. An apostle is one who has "paradoxically something new to contribute,"[29] a divine doctrine. Yet Adler denies that he has any new doctrine to contribute, insisting that he does not regard his *Sermons* as "revelations alongside of or over against Christianity."[30] Rather, Adler describes his experience as one of being "rescued in a miraculous way."[31] It was, he says, a deeply moving religious experience in which he was emotionally seized and awakened. However, as Kierkegaard points out:

> The emotional seizure of the individual by something higher is far from defining a Christian adequately, for by emotion may be expressed a pagan view, pagan conceptions of God. In order to express oneself Christianly there is required, besides the more universal language of the heart, also skill and schooling in the definition of Christian concepts, while at the same time it is of course assumed that the emotion is of a specific, qualitative sort, the Christian emotion.[32]

Adler, who was not in this stricter sense seized by a Christian emotion, expresses himself in a language that stands in no relation to a proper Christian understanding. As a result he speaks "like one who talks too fast and does not articulate clearly . . . it is twaddle."[33] As Kierkegaard explains: "For a Christian awakening what is required, on the one hand, is being grasped in a Christian sense and, on the other hand, conceptual and terminological firmness and definiteness."[34] It is precisely this conceptual firmness that Adler lacks:

> If from an earlier time Magister A. had had a strict schooling in the concepts, a veneration for the dogmatic, qualitative concept of "a revelation," he would have had something to resist

with, something to hold on to, something that might prevent
the precipitate utterance. But, unfortunately, Magister A. is a
Hegelian. So there can be no hope that something might save
him from the confusion, since the whole of his philosophic
learning must precisely confirm him in the notion that altogether correctly and with philosophic precision he expresses
his subjective change by the invention that he had had a revelation.[35]

Adler's speculative understanding of Christian concepts has deprived him
of the possibility of understanding what it means to be called by a revelation. His problem is that he "is not in possession of one single presupposition which would make him inwardly aware of the fact that this philosophy totally confuses Christianity . . ."[36] He lacks a proper grounding in
Christian dogmatic concepts.

The depth of Adler's religious confusion is evident in the fact that he
begins with a definite claim to revelation, but afterwards changes his claim
without apparently being aware of the contradiction. Furthermore, Adler
not only changes his claim from being entrusted with a new doctrine to being
rescued in a miraculous way,[37] but he also changes the category of his claim
from the religious to the aesthetic. For though he now denies that he is an
apostle with a new doctrine to communicate, he suggests that he is really
a genius. The content of his alleged revelation is now to be understood as
the combined product of divine inspiration and intellectual achievement.
Kierkegaard addresses this confusion of categories by examining what he
calls the "qualitative difference between an apostle and a genius."[38]

GENIUS AND APOSTOLIC AUTHORITY

Christian revelation is posited as a paradoxically new point of departure
for the human understanding of self and God. Moreover, the authority of
that revelation is posited as a transcendent authority, which is not reduc-
ible to any immanent form of authority. By "immanent," Kierkegaard
means that which is relative and transient in nature: "In the sphere of
immanence . . . authority is only a transient, vanishing factor, which either
vanishes later in temporal existence, or vanishes for the fact that earthly
life itself is a transitory factor, which vanishes with all its differences."[39] It
follows that all authority relationships in the sphere of immanence are
conditioned by a set of limiting factors. The authority of genius, for exam-

ple, is relative to the native intellectual capacity one possesses from birth, and is developed to a greater or lesser degree in any individual depending on a variety of external factors. Similarly, the authority possessed by a hereditary monarch is relative to the accidental fact of being born to a certain family in a certain time. Furthermore, the authority possessed by. geniuses and monarchs is limited by the fact that neither can exceed the finite period of a lifetime. By contrast, divine authority remains the same throughout eternity. Though one can perhaps console oneself with the thought that one is not forever bound to the authority of a king, this cannot be thought with respect to divine authority, which is eternal and irrevocable.[40]

The main difference between the genius and the apostle can thus be summarized in the following way. The genius takes his point of departure in immanence, he does not rise above the purely human order of things. The creativity of his genius flows directly from his own personality. Though he may have something new to contribute, "this newness vanishes again in its gradual assimilation by the race, just as the distinction 'genius' vanishes when one thinks of eternity."[41] Kierkegaard here calls attention to the etymological meaning of the word: from the Latin *ingenium*, meaning that which is inborn.[42] Genius is an accidental property that gives one a natural but relative advantage over others, and therefore something that must be "appraised purely on aesthetic grounds, according to the content and specific gravity his productions are found to have."[43]

The apostle, however, who takes his point of departure in transcendence, is the 'exception.' He is what he is not by virtue of a certain natural endowment he enjoys over others, but by reason of his divine authority. "The apostle has paradoxically something new to contribute, the newness of which, precisely because it is paradoxical and not an anticipation of what may eventually be developed in the race, remains constant."[44] Kierkegaard draws our attention here to the etymological meaning of the word *apostle:* from the Greek *apostolia*, meaning one who is sent forth. This definition captures the idea that the apostle is a messenger in the service of God. As Kierkegaard puts it: "An apostle is not born, an apostle is a man called and sent by God, sent by him on a mission."[45] It is not possible, therefore, to determine whether one is an apostle on the basis of an aesthetic or philosophical appraisal of his doctrine. "The order of the sequence is exactly the reverse: the man called by a revelation, to whom was entrusted a doctrine, argues from the fact that this was a revelation, from the fact that he has authority."[46]

Kierkegaard explicates the logic of apostolic authority by comparing it to the way we recognize legitimate forms of mundane authority. For example, a military officer speaks and acts with authority, and his orders must be executed without hesitation by those who acknowledge him as an authority. The conditions for this authority consist in the established chain of military command, which in turn is grounded in the authority of the state.[47] But suppose that this same officer now orders a civilian to do something. One might well imagine that the civilian will feel no special compulsion to obey, since he does not acknowledge the officer as an authority. As Kierkegaard writes: "When the man who has the authority to say it says 'Go!' and when he who has not authority says, 'Go!'–then indeed the saying 'Go' along with its content is identical; appraised aesthetically, if you will, they are both equally well said, but the authority makes the difference."[48]

According to Kierkegaard, authority itself must be distinguished from the personal features of its bearer, for it is "a specific quality which comes from another place and makes itself felt precisely when the content of the saying or of the action is assumed to be indifferent."[49] To inquire as to whether an authority is profound or clever is therefore an impertinence that undermines obedience:

> A king is indeed assumed to have authority. Why is it then that one is almost offended at learning that a king is clever, is an artist, etc.? Surely it is because in his case one essentially accentuates the royal authority, and in comparison with this the commoner qualification of human difference is a vanishing factor, is unessential, a disturbing accident. . . . To ask whether the king is a genius, with the implication that in such case he is to be obeyed, is really lese-majeste, for the question contains a doubt concerning subjection to authority. . . . To honor one's father because he is a distinguished pate is impiety.[50]

This is especially true in the case of religious authority. To obey an apostle on account of the profundity of his doctrine is to accept orthodoxy by accentuating something that is entirely beside the point. Moreover, the very question of whether a doctrine is profound betrays a doubt concerning the legitimacy of the authority. It assumes that there may be objective grounds on which to determine whether the authority is genuine. But because the apostle's authority is dialectically conditioned by its appeal to a transcendent revelation, he stands in a paradoxical relation to all others. The apostle cannot prove that he has divine authority any more than

Christ could prove that he was divine. As Kierkegaard observes: "He has no other proof but his own assertion. And thus precisely it ought to be, for otherwise the believer would come into a direct relation to him, not into a paradoxical relationship."[51]

The comparison with immanent forms of authority brings out a further feature of the logic of apostolic authority. In the sphere of immanence, it is always reasonable to inquire into the conditions under which an authority exists. The authority of a military officer is conditioned by the whole chain of military command, which in turn is conditioned by the authority of the state. The apostle, however, bears no sensible marks of divine authority.[52] Indeed, if there could be sensible certitude of the fact that one was an apostle, then this would *eo ipso* show that one was precisely not an apostle.[53] Even the alleged performance of miracles can give rise only to a heightened offense, since one accepts the miracle only if one believes that the other really has divine authority, and this must be believed on faith.

Though it may be true to say that the apostle Paul possessed a rare insight into the nature of faith, this form of appraisal does not even approximate the acknowledgment that he is an apostle called by God and vested with divine authority. Paul's authority is a quality that cannot be assimilated to the class of purely human attributes, for it is posited from outside the human order of things. Divine authority is not something that can be delegated by any human office.[54] It is not to be regarded as a natural human capacity which can be realized in the development of a human being, and hence it cannot be classified in the category of possible human achievements. Divine authority, like faith, is something that can be exercised only through the agency of divine grace.

Kierkegaard draws from this the conclusion that anyone who receives divine authority must conduct himself in a manner that reflects an awareness of his paradoxical situation. The apostle must not appeal to cleverness, "for then he is a fool; he must not enter into a purely aesthetic or philosophic discussion about the content of his doctrine, for then he is *distrait*. No, he must appeal to his divine authority, and precisely by that, while he is willing to sacrifice life and all, he must *prevent* all aesthetic and philosophically direct objections against the content or form of the doctrine."[55] The task of the true religious authority is to be transparent in God. The authority of the apostle lies not in his originality, in his knowledge, or in any other purely human qualification, but in his *de facto* embodiment of those ideals and values approved by God. As one author points out, "religious authority is a force that one individual holds over another in virtue of the latter's opinion that the former is a true representative of the deity. It is personal and deontic and incapable of objective verification."[56]

The main philosophical dispute concerning authority and revelation is whether and under what conditions the claim to divine authority is justifiable. Since we can get nowhere by demanding empirical justification, the Christian view of revelation appears to beg the question at this crucial point. But this is not an accurate accounting of the matter. For the point is not that one could be *justified* in believing the apostle on the grounds that he has divine authority. This would indeed be circular. In fact, one is never justified in believing that he has divine authority, at least not on empirical grounds. Here there is no circularity, for one merely affirms the fact that it is impossible to have a sensible certitude of a transcendent authority. One must either acknowledge that this authority exists and is binding on one's life, or else reject it.

But to say that the value of divine authority cannot be immediately recognized is not to say that one must accept it blindly. As T. H. Croxall points out:

> Are we then to accept the Apostolic authority blindly? By no means. We must examine why we accept it, and also its objective content. But in the last resort we must leave dialectic aside and submit, before we can know the value of Apostolic authority. For Christianity is communicated and kept alive not epistemologically but existentially.[57]

Kierkegaard emphatically affirms that Christianity is an existence communication, brought into the world by the use of authority.[58] Divine revelation does not present itself for human judgment, but points the way to a higher truth. But this does not mean that we are unable to examine the objective content of the revelation, or our reasons for accepting it:

> People say that faith rests upon authority, and think that they have thereby excluded dialectics, but this is not so. For dialectics begin by asking how it is that one abandons oneself to this authority; whether one can understand why one chose it, or whether it was an accident. In the latter case, it was not authority, not even for the believer, if he knows it was accidental.[59]

For all that Kierkegaard has written about the paradoxical nature of the object of faith, the decision to accept Christian revelation as authoritative is neither blind nor irrational. Indeed, Kierkegaard's analysis of the case of Adler suggests several criteria that one can use to determine the consistency of an appeal to Christian authority.

THE CRITERIA OF RELIGIOUS AUTHORITY

We begin with the form of the Christ-revelation. According to Kierkegaard's analysis, this is an existential communication, through which we are taught that our self-centered nature is absolutely unlike that of God's divine nature. Truth is revealed in the form of a teacher who is the embodiment of the truth, and the task of faith is to strive to reduplicate that truth in one's own life. Christian revelation demands that the individual renounce self-interest and the things of this world. As a transcendent authority, revelation presents itself as an absolute judgment on the human conception of what is true and good.

The marks of an authentic revelation must therefore be determined in accordance with the standard set by the Christ-revelation. As Julia Watkin notes in her introduction to the Danish edition of the book on Adler,[60] the true religious exception will not only have been entrusted with a new doctrine to communicate, but he will act in the service of God and devote his life entirely to the mission upon which he has been sent. Such a person will speak with divine authority, calling attention to the revelation as his justification. Furthermore, he will be a witness of unusual conviction, prepared to endure ridicule and personal sacrifice for the sake of the truth.

Because of the inherently paradoxical nature of divine revelation, the religious exception will have to take conscious possession of his call. As Kierkegaard explains:

> The called person in our age will not merely be the instrument (spontaneous) but will consciously take possession of his call in quite another sense than what always has been the case in a divine call–to make up his mind about and to understand himself in this extraordinary thing that has happened to him. . . . His responsibility in reflection would then be that he not become the worst misfortune for the established order and that in fear and trembling he see to it, as far as he is able, that no one is harmed by a direct relationship to his extraordinariness.[61]

We expect that such a person will handle his task in a thoughtful and intelligent manner, and that his desire to reform will be motivated by a genuine love for the established order.[62] Understanding the true nature of his mission, he will discourage thoughtless imitation of his action, encouraging others to seek the truth for themselves. He will not shrink from opposition, as Watkin further points out, because he will always fear the possibility that he might have misunderstood the divine message.[63] The opposition of the establishment will prevent him from taking his position for granted, and serve to remind him of the paradoxical relationship he bears to the revelation he has received.

Adler, by contrast, has no new doctrine to communicate. His words and actions do not indicate that he is a man with a divine mission, or that he is motivated by a genuine concern for the welfare of others. His conduct suggests rather that he is interested in attracting attention to himself. When subjected to the scrutiny of the church authorities, Adler does not stand firm and speak from a deep inner conviction; he does not speak with divine authority. Far from being prepared to endure the slightest opposition from the establishment, Adler seeks to justify himself by appealing to aesthetic categories—further proof of his religious confusion.

Adler lacks the dialectical qualifications necessary to carry out the Christian mission to preach and clarify the word of God. Thus, he is not only unprepared to fulfill the duties and obligations of an ordained minister, but he also poses a real threat to the religious establishment as a disseminator of false attitudes and beliefs about Christianity. Adler's fault lies in the fact that he did not give himself sufficient time to try to understand himself in relation to his conversion experience. But Kierkegaard also shows that the case of Adler is symptomatic of a much deeper religious confusion afflicting the age as a whole. For that an ordained minister should be ignorant of Christian concepts and the appropriate means for testing his own experience against them indicates that Christian theology has lost sight of the very dogmatic presuppositions on which it rests.

Kierkegaard suggests that Adler is a fitting epigram on Christendom, precisely because he was permitted to become an ordained minister even though he professed a philosophical conception of Christianity that reduced it to something unchristian and devoid of ethical content.[64] Similarly, he suggests that Adler is an unconscious satire on the Hegelian philosophy of the day. For although Adler renounced his allegiance to that philosophy, he continued to explain his experience in the language of speculative idealism, thereby demonstrating its ethical and religious inadequacies.[65]

The case of Adler represents a clear conceptual link between Kierkegaard's critique of Hegelianism and his attack on Christendom. For as the analysis in *On Authority and Revelation* shows, the language of orthodox Christian theology has been so corrupted by the influence of speculative philosophy that it no longer has the power to shape the subjectivity of the believer. Christian speculation undermines the very possibility of reaching a qualitative decision in the religious sphere, and hence, the possibility of realizing authentic Christian faith. Moreover, it poses a grave threat to the possibility of educating about Christianity. In this way, Kierkegaard brings us to the very heart of the problem initially posed by Climacus in the *Postscript*, namely, the problem of becoming a Christian in Christendom.

8

❧❧

The Dialectic of Religious Communication

No examination of Kierkegaard's conception of revelation can be complete without a discussion of his understanding and use of indirect communication. In what follows I shall examine the presuppositions underlying Kierkegaard's use of indirect discourse. I am not concerned here with the various devices of indirect communication (metaphor, irony, humor, etc.), since these have been amply documented in the work of others. The major focus will be on Kierkegaard's outlines for two lectures on communication composed in 1847.[1] These lectures provide us with a comprehensive discussion of the central ideas underlying the general theory of communication.

THE ETHICS OF COMMUNICATION

The argument for the appropriateness of the indirect form of discourse is based on a distinction between two ways of knowing. All knowledge, according to Kierkegaard, can be divided into two general types: knowledge that is about something ("knowledge-that") and self-knowledge.[2] The former type of knowledge is of a factual nature, and hence characteristic of the sciences and scholarship.[3] It requires a relevant assertion of truth as well as the possession of appropriate evidential support. By contrast, self-knowledge does not take as its object "the pure self-consciousness and the pure I."[4] It is knowledge of the self in the Socratic sense, in which one comes to 'know oneself' through the process of self-reflection and choice. In the *Postscript* he calls this "essential" knowledge, which is defined in the following way:

> All essential knowledge relates to existence or only such knowledge as has an essential relationship to existence is essential knowledge. All knowledge which does not inwardly relate itself to existence, in the reflection of inwardness is, essentially viewed, accidental knowledge; its degree and scope is essentially different.[5]

The sort of knowledge Kierkegaard calls essential is closely related to the activities of reflection and choice. This point is brought out in *Either/Or,* where it is explained that the ethical individual "knows himself, but this knowing is not simply contemplation . . . it is a collecting of oneself, which itself is an action, and this is why I have with aforethought used the expression 'to choose oneself' instead of 'to know oneself.'"[6] It is by adopting a principle of practice that I give sense to my actuality and direction to my possibilities. Essential knowledge, or questions that give rise to essential knowledge, must generate an imperative to act, to break out of the chain of abstract contemplation: "The real action is not the external act, but an internal decision in which the individual puts an end to the mere possibility and identifies himself with the content of his thought in order to exist in it. This is the action."[7] What this involves is the transformation of a conceptualization into an actuality. One must not merely think about the kind of person one wants to be, one must become that person. Kierkegaard expresses this in the form of an ethical requirement: "Ethics concentrates upon the individual, and ethically it is the task of every individual to become an entire [human being]. . . . Whether anyone realizes his task or not makes no difference, the fact that the requirement is there is the important thing."[8] And further down, he makes the following Kantian observation: "Whatever is great in the sphere of the universally human must therefore not be communicated as a subject for admiration, but as an ethical requirement."[9] The ethical task lies with the individual.

As we have seen, Christian faith requires that the believer resolve inwardly to accept Christ as the truth and to bring his life into conformity with the ideal exemplified by Christ's pattern. The Christian must acknowledge that he is separated from God by sin and can find salvation only by entering into a relationship with God in time. But God can be present to the existing individual only in the ethical-religious striving of faith, where the individual strives to reduplicate the ideality of Christ in his own existence.[10] Kierkegaard expresses this by saying that "the absolute *telos* exists for the individual only when he yields it an absolute devotion,"[11] and that "the absolute good has the remarkable trait of being definable solely in terms of the mode of acquisition."[12] The mode of acquisition appropriate to Christianity is always in the medium of actuality: "Christianity tends above all toward actuality, toward being made actual, the only medium to which it is truly related. It is not to be possessed in any way other than by being made actual."[13] By showing that Christianity is preeminently concerned with existence, and that the existing individual can be related to God only by making God actual in his existence, the life of faith must be understood in terms of becoming.[14] All attempts to mediate Christianity in the sphere of possibility—to mediate the relationship to God by way of an intellectual movement—must be accounted a failure to fulfill the ethical-religious requirement imposed by the Christ-revelation. Hence Kierkegaard's observation that "the resolved individual does not even wish to know anything more about this *telos* than that it exists, for as soon as he acquires some knowledge about it, he already begins to be retarded in his striving."[15]

According to Kierkegaard, the absolute good cannot be quantified. It imposes an absolute *telos* on the existing individual's existence, which is to say that its requirement is unconditional and must be willed in every moment.[16] Because "an eternal happiness is a *telos* for existing individuals, these two (the absolute end and the existing individual) cannot be conceived as realizing a union in existence in terms of rest."[17] What this means is that no less than "the whole of time and of existence should be the period of striving."[18] It is clear, then, why Kierkegaard regards abstract speculation as inimical to faith. For if the relationship to the absolute *telos* is not realized in the actuality of the individual's own existence, then it does not exist.[19] To claim that one has objective knowledge of the absolute *telos* is a contradiction in terms, and any attempt to be related to the absolute *telos* on objective grounds (i.e., intellectually) must fail. Thus Kierkegaard affirms that "objective thinking, when it ranks as highest, is precisely irreligious."[20]

In terms of the pragmatist conception of faith I have ascribed to Kierkegaard, the absolute paradox forces the realization that the only way to be related to the truth of revelation is through a process of ethical-religious striving. The object of Christian faith is not a doctrine; it is the teacher, who embodies the ideal pattern of the Christian life. The proper response to revelation is not mere doctrinal assent, but an obedient response to the absolute requirement that one recognizes to be binding on one's life. But this raises questions about the dialectic of religious communication, not only from the point of view of one who wishes to communicate something about one's faith, but also from the point of view of revelation itself.

Kierkegaard divides all communication into two main forms. On the one hand, there is the communication of objective knowledge, which can be shared directly with others through the medium of common ideas. On the other hand, there is the communication of subjective or essential knowledge, which exists only in the medium of actuality, and hence cannot be shared directly with others. Subjective or essential knowledge, which is of an ethical nature, must be communicated as an art.[21]

Kierkegaard offers two reasons why essential knowledge cannot be communicated directly. The first is that such knowledge refers to existence, which is a continual process of becoming and cannot be communicated directly to others without thereby falsifying it. The second reason is that ethical knowledge is innate. Every human being possesses the capacity to attain essential knowledge for himself.[22] It is therefore not something that can be acquired through a direct communication, but something that must be realized.[23]

Kierkegaard illustrates these points with the example of a country boy who has the innate capacity to become a soldier, a potential that can be brought out by drill and practice:

> The military assumes that every country boy who joins the army possesses the necessary capacities to develop into a soldier. . . . Now the communication begins. The corporal doesn't explain to the soldier what it is to drill, etc.; he communicates it to him as an art. He teaches him to use the abilities and potential so that they are actualized. And this is the way the ethical is communicated. . . . The object of communication is consequently not an objective knowledge but a realization.[24]

In so far as the ethical is something that must be given expression in a life, it cannot be taught or communicated like a science. External conditions are insufficient to make one a moral person; something more is required. That 'something more' is what Kierkegaard calls the decisiveness of inwardness.

According to Kierkegaard, every communication has four parts: the communicator, the receiver, the object of the communication, and the communication itself.[25] But when the object of the communication is the ethical, the dialectic of the communication changes in three important respects. First, the object of the communication drops out, for if everyone knows it, then it is unethical to attempt to communicate it. Next, the communicator drops out, since there is no need to communicate anything. And finally, the receiver drops out, for there is now neither a communicator nor an object of communication. What then is the status of the communication of the ethical? Kierkegaard says there remains only one true communicator of the ethical, namely, God. "In regard to the ethical . . . every man relates himself as an apprentice to God, who is the master-teacher."[26]

But how does God communicate with us in an ethical way? He uses midwives. The Christian midwife is one who gives rise to the birth of a new person by being the occasion for that person to acquire essential knowledge. This is the mode of communication employed by Kierkegaard in the authorship. The objective of the maieutic method is to get others to look inward, to become self-reflective. As Walter Lowrie points out, the maieutic is "artfully devised to prompt the other to think out the thing for himself, while the subjectivity of the communicator remains concealed."[27] Whereas Socrates used the maieutic method to bring out latent knowledge in others, Kierkegaard uses it to stimulate others to action.

Kierkegaard's objective is to get the reader to see that it is necessary to separate religious categories from aesthetic ones, to resign from false concerns such as objective knowledge and public opinion. He wants to get the reader to rediscover his essential primitivity:

> Every human existence (*Existents*) ought to have primitivity. But the primitive existence always contains a reexamination of the fundamental. . . . This is honesty in the deepest sense. Completely to lack primitivity and consequently reexamination, to accept everything automatically as common practice and let it suffice that it is common practice, consequently to evade responsibility for doing likewise—this is dishonesty.[28]

Kierkegaard is aware that if he is to get others to be honest about where they stand in relation to existence and to God, he must inspire them with concern and unrest. Indeed, this is the very most that one can do.[29] Kierkegaard cannot give others the experience of appropriating the truth in the passion of inwardness, for this can only be achieved by the individual in the passion of subjectivity.

THE INCARNATION AS INDIRECT COMMUNICATION

In the following passage from *Practice in Christianity*, Kierkegaard explains that the Christ-revelation contains a necessary indirection, an indirection which is essentially rooted in the absolute paradox:

> If someone says directly: I am God; the Father and I are one, this is direct communication. But if the person who says it, the communicator, is this individual human being, an individual human being just like others, then this communication is not quite entirely direct, because it is not entirely direct that an individual human being should be God—whereas what he says is entirely direct. Because of the communicator the communication contains a contradiction, it becomes an indirect communication; it confronts you with a choice: whether you will believe him or not.[30]

It is indeed true that Christ spoke directly to his disciples, and that they in turn spoke directly to others about the Christ-revelation. But this direct form of communication is qualified by the fact that Christ is the absolute paradox. Though Christ communicates directly when he proclaims his divinity, he is, by all appearances, a lowly and insignificant man. His direct communication is made indirect by virtue of the fact that he is "a sign of contradiction":

> To be a sign of contradiction is to be a something else that stands in contrast to what one immediately is. So it is with the God-man. Immediately, he is an individual human being, just like others, a lowly, unimpressive human being, but now comes the contradiction—that *he* is God.[31]

And further down he explains that the God-man, as the sign of contradiction, cannot possibly communicate himself directly. All the empirical evidence militates against the truth of what he says. It is only by leaving out the communicator, and hence the absolute paradox, that the modern age has succeeded in transforming Christianity into a direct communication.[32]

Properly understood, Christianity can neither be communicated directly nor accepted immediately on objective grounds. Christ does not present the truth in the form of a doctrine. Revelation is an "existential communication," that is, the truth of Christianity is embodied in the life of the teacher:

> Christianity is not a doctrine but an existential communication expressing an existential contradiction. If Christianity were a doctrine it would *eo ipso* not be an opposite to speculative thought, but rather a phase within it. . . . Precisely because

Christianity is not a doctrine it exhibits the principle, as was noted above, that there is a tremendous difference between knowing what Christianity is and being a Christian.[33]

Kierkegaard points out that Christianity has declared itself a paradox, in order to "prevent anyone from misguidedly entering upon the objective way."[34] The salient point is that faith is not merely a matter for understanding, it makes every individual unconditionally responsible for his own ethical development. Moreover, for that individual who is interested in his eternal happiness, the paradox of the God-man creates the greatest possible concern and unrest. He confronts every individual with the challenge of discipleship. He has no truth to give, no doctrine; he communicates the truth with his life. "In relation to an existential communication, existing in it is the maximum of attainment, and understanding it is merely an evasion of the task."[35]

PHILOSOPHY AND THE LIMITS OF COMMUNICATION

The foregoing is a sketch of Kierkegaard's theory of communication. We have seen how it applies both to his purposes in the authorship and to his understanding of Christian revelation, which is also a form of indirect communication. I shall now consider some criticisms that may be raised against Kierkegaard's position.

In an article entitled "The Limitations of Religious Existentialism," John A. Mourant raises a number of difficulties for Kierkegaard's theory of communication.[36] He begins by noting the connection between the indirect form of communication and subjective truth:

> For Kierkegaard the problem of communication is bound up with that of truth. As is well known, he proclaimed the subjectivity of truth. He was convinced that what he termed the essential truth, religious truth, is subjective, inward, concealed, and secret. As such it cannot be shared with others nor communicated directly to them. . . . Here we are in the world of essences and communication is based, as Kierkegaard would say, on the "security of social continuity," whereas religious truth concerns the existence of the individual and his relation to God, a relationship which cannot be shared with another. As Kierkegaard puts it: "A direct relationship between one spiri-

tual being and another with respect to the essential truth is unthinkable."[37]

It will be recalled that Kierkegaard defines subjective truth as a way of being, a form of life, something which is reflected in the process of existing. 'Becoming' is, for Kierkegaard, the basic existential category. Subjective truth, which is related to becoming, requires an existential appropriation.[38] Since subjective truth is an existence, and existence is a continual process of becoming, such truth cannot be directly communicated without thereby falsifying it. As Kierkegaard explains: "Precisely because he himself is constantly in process of becoming inwardly or in inwardness, the religious individual can never use direct communication, the movement in him being the precise opposite of that presupposed in direct communication."[39]

Given that the direct form of communication deals in truth that is objective and can be shared with others through the medium of universal ideas, and that indirect communication deals in truth that is subjective and cannot be shared directly with others, it is necessary to consider two problems: "First, why should there be any indirect communication, what motive or motives can we assign for it? Secondly, just how can a religious or existential truth, a truth appropriated by each individual for himself, be communicated?"[40]

The first question asks why anyone who possesses the passion of the infinite should feel compelled to communicate that truth to others. Mourant suggests that Kierkegaard may have a personal as well as a religious reason. As for the personal reason, Mourant sees a parallel between Kierkegaard's own religious development and his mode of communication. The melancholy of the early years is seen to become gradually transformed into an intense religious feeling that finally causes him to abandon the indirect approach of the pseudonyms in favor of a more direct form of address.[41] As we saw in the first chapter, this psychologistic explanation is discredited by the fact that even the earliest pseudonymous works were accompanied by 'edifying discourses,' purely religious works that Kierkegaard composed in a direct style and published under his own name.

Kierkegaard does, however, offer the following personal reason for undertaking the authorship:

> I do not say that I am an outstanding Christian. . . . But I do maintain that I know with uncommon clarity and definiteness what Christianity is, what can be required of the Christian,

what it means to be Christian. To an unusual degree I have, I believe, the qualifications to portray this. I also believe it is my duty to do it, simply because it seems to be forgotten in Christendom, and obviously there is no probability that the present generation is capable of educating in Christianity.[42]

Kierkegaard sees it as his mission to get others to choose the good, to become ethical and religious beings who fulfill their *telos*. But in Christendom, those who profess to have Christian salvation as their *telos* fail to understand the ethical-religious requirements this imposes on their lives. In Christendom, people live under the illusion that they are Christians, when in fact they do not live their lives in Christian categories. Kierkegaard therefore sets out to combat this illusion by reintroducing Christianity into Christendom.

There is also, as Mourant correctly points out, a religious motivation behind the authorship. For Kierkegaard was not merely a dialectician or literary stylist, he was a theological candidate with the legal authority to preach, and he accepted Christianity as *objectively* true.[43] But to Mourant, this suggests a certain ambivalence in Kierkegaard's religious attitude: "At times his Christianity appears quite objective, doctrinal, and orthodox; at other times, he is in rebellion against his Church and teaches a Christianity that is something wholly subjective and impossible to communicate precisely because it is in his eyes essentially a way of life that must be appropriated personally by each individual and identified with his own being."[44] Is it possible, given Kierkegaard's understanding of faith, to accept Christianity as an objective truth while insisting on its essential subjectivity?

Some careful distinctions have to be made. First of all, there is a significant difference between asserting that one accepts Christianity as objectively true and that one accepts Christianity as true on the strength of objective evidence. Kierkegaard insists throughout that it is impossible to determine the truth of Christianity on objective grounds. This does not mean, however, that one cannot accept Christianity as objectively true. There is, as we have seen, a pragmatic justification for accepting Christianity.

A second distinction concerns the sense in which Kierkegaard conceives of objective doctrinal orthodoxy. As we saw earlier, the objective doctrinal content of Christianity is grounded in revelation. Dogmatic Christian concepts are defined by reference to the objective standard of the Christ-revelation. This is what Kierkegaard means when he says it is possible to have objective knowledge about Christianity, and that it is possible to communicate this knowledge in a direct fashion. But even though

Christian doctrine thus forms the objective basis of the religious community, it does not 'contain' the truth of Christianity. Kierkegaard constantly stresses the point that religious truth exists only in the medium of actuality: "Christianity tends above all toward actuality, toward being made actual, the only medium to which it is truly related. It is not to be possessed in any way other than being made actual."[45] He concludes from this that the truth of Christianity must be communicated as an essential truth, that is, a truth that exists only in its appropriation by an existing individual, and that any attempt to communicate that truth directly (in the absence of double reflection) involves a deception.[46]

The second difficulty raised by Mourant has to do with the mode of the indirect communication. Given the assumption that the truth of Christianity is an existence, it would seem that there can be no finality to the process of indirect communication. And indeed, the maieutic method employed by Kierkegaard in the authorship can never be final. However, once the communicator reaches the religious stage of existence, indirect communication is characterized by the reduplication in the individual of those truths which he believes. In the words of Anti-Climacus: "Any communication concerning existing requires a communicator; in other words, the communicator is the reduplication of the communication; to exist in what one understands is to reduplicate."[47] This is, once again, the central point about essential knowledge: it is not objective knowledge, but a knowledge that is grounded in an active process of self-realization. The communicator of the ethical must therefore become what he would communicate.

The highest form of communication in the sphere of Christianity is therefore the act of "bearing witness." But according to Mourant, there is an inner contradiction in the thought of Kierkegaard on this point:

> "Bearing witness" is not so much a final result of the process of communication in which the individual possesses the objective truth of revelation, for truth is inwardness, subjectivity, and becoming, but rather a return of the dialectic upon itself in that by "bearing witness," by suffering, persecution, etc., the individual calls attention once more to himself, endeavoring to make others take notice by another and perhaps more "artful method" than that of the pseudonymous works.[48]

In reply to this concern it must be reiterated that Kierkegaard does not attempt to communicate the subjective truth of Christianity. To say that "bearing witness" is the highest or final stage of communication in the sphere of Christianity is not to say that this involves a direct transmission of the truth of Christianity. Bearing Witness to the truth of Christianity may involve a communication of the results of one's own appropriation of the truth, but this can serve only as a way of inspiring and edifying others, causing them to take notice. The communicator in the religious stage of existence is a witness to the truth of Christianity with his entire life, that is, both in word and action. Just as Socrates, by wagering his existence on the possibility of immortality, was a witness to the truth of immortality (Kierkegaard calls this a "proof"), so the believer in Christianity must be a witness to the truth of Christian salvation by "so determining the pattern of his life that it must be found acceptable."[49]

Commenting on Kierkegaard's view of sermonic discourse, Paul L. Holmer writes: "In a discourse, actually delivered before the Holy Communion, Kierkegaard says that it 'would merely give thee pause for an instant on the way to the altar,' but then he adds a pregnant comment: 'It is true that a sermon should also bear witness to Him, proclaiming His word and His teaching, but for all that a sermon is not His voice.'"[50] I understand Kierkegaard to mean that the sermon cannot establish certainty for the listener. Although the sermon does presuppose a certainty on the part of the preacher, this certainty is not a consequence of proofs, but a certainty of faith which is reflected in the preacher's words and actions. Though the sermon is admittedly a direct form of religious discourse, it must be distinguished from the ordinary direct form of discourse. Holmer expresses this by saying that the sermon is not to be confused with a lecture:

> In the latter, agreement or disagreement is the aim. What the lecturer asks is that the hearer recognize and recognize for himself what has been said. If the sentences in a lecture are true, they are then worthy of being learned. The immediate assent is then important. But when a sermon is professed to stand in an analogous relation to the worshiper, the categories are confused. For a sermon is not something to be learned even if, like the occasional lecture, it may be true. The religious response is not an assent to the truth of the sermon. This is why Kierkegaard's authors say over and over that a sermon is not His voice and that one is not saved by the discourse.[51]

The point of the sermon must be to get the hearer to achieve reduplication and to *exist* in the truth.

This brings us to a further difficulty raised by Mourant. If "bearing witness" is aimed only at getting another to achieve reduplication and to exist in the truth, then what assurance can there be that this has been accomplished? It will be recalled that the criterion of authentic Christianity is, according to Kierkegaard, the pattern of the humble, serving Christ, who reveals the true nature of God to man. Christ presents the ideal ethical-religious pattern for reduplication by every individual. It is with reference to this ideal standard that Kierkegaard clarifies the proper ethical understanding of Christian concepts, and is able to establish the criteria of authentic Christianity. By the application of these criteria it is possible to determine whether a person has a proper grasp of Christian concepts. There is thus a limited sense in which it will be possible to determine whether or not the communication of these concepts has been successful. Indeed, Kierkegaard's treatment of the case of Adler presupposes that this must be possible.

It should be noted in this connection that even though Kierkegaard admits the possibility of knowing objectively what Christianity is, he is careful to add that "whether one himself is [a true Christian] cannot be *known*, surely not with definiteness–it must be believed, and in faith there is always fear and trembling."[52] It is not possible to know whether one is in fact related to the eternal, or whether one is in fact saved. The life of faith is a necessary but not a sufficient condition for being accepted by God as a Christian.

Commenting on the Christian purpose of his authorship, Kierkegaard says that it was his primary task to present in every way the ideal picture of being a Christian, that is, to illuminate Christ as the ideal pattern and the object of faith.[53] He considers himself eminently qualified to do this because he "knows with uncommon clarity and definiteness what Christianity is, what can be required of the Christian, what it means to be Christian."[54] He also refers to this task as a duty, "simply because it seems to be forgotten in Christendom, and obviously there is no probability that the present generation is capable of educating in Christianity."[55] The purpose of the authorship, according to Kierkegaard, is to regain clarity with respect to dogmatic Christian concepts, to make it possible once again to "educate in Christianity." This purpose is clearly reflected in the writings of Climacus and in the book on Adler, where Kierkegaard is concerned with exposing the conceptual confusion that has caused the age to lose sight of Christian concepts and their decisive significance for the Christian life. It has been my contention that this constitutes the philosophical content of the authorship.

However, in so far as it is Kierkegaard's purpose in the authorship to confront the individual with "the most decisive definitions of the religious," in order that he might "come to his senses and realize what is implied in calling himself Christian,"[56] to get the reader to achieve reduplication and to exist in the truth, it would seem that he makes use of a *direct* form of communication. The philosophical component in the works we have been considering constitutes a direct form of discourse. But if this is the case, then how does Kierkegaard reconcile the need for a direct form of communication (education) concerning dogmatic Christian concepts with his emphasis on the necessity of indirect communication in ethical-religious matters?

This problem is given a very precise formulation by Harry S. Broudy, who claims that if Kierkegaard is right about the impossibility of communicating existence directly, then

> philosophy is faced with a dilemma: if it sticks to the ideal of objectivity, it cannot communicate human existence; if it wants to describe and communicate the truth about human existence, it has to abandon the ideal of objectivity and resort to modes of communication whose cognitive status in philosophy is suspect.[57]

Is Kierkegaard inconsistent on this point, or is it possible to reconcile these apparently opposite tendencies within the authorship? In order for Kierkegaard to be guilty of an inconsistency, it would have to be shown either that he attempts to communicate human existence, or that the authorship as a whole constitutes a direct communication when viewed from the standpoint of its avowed Christian purpose. Textual evidence militates strongly against the suggestion that Kierkegaard may have attempted to communicate human existence. In fact, his philosophical inquiries are intended to demonstrate the limits of communication in relation to existence. However, if the direct communication of a philosophical result is required to make this point, and indeed, to accomplish the wider Christian purpose claimed for the authorship, then it would seem that the dominant mode of communication is direct rather than indirect.

I want to suggest that there are really two levels of communication in the authorship. Kierkegaard preserves the essential indirection of the pseudonymous works through the use of metaphor, irony, humor, polemic, and pseudonymity. On another level, he sets forth theses, and defends them with sound logical argument based on careful conceptual analysis. But this second level of communication, which is admittedly direct, occurs *within* the larger indirect framework of the authorship. Nowhere is this more clearly in evidence than in the Climacus writings. There, the reader encounters at once the indirection of Climacus's pseudonymity, an indirection that is reinforced by his own admission that he is not a Christian and that his whole project is to be understood merely as a thought experiment. Yet he is at the same time one who professes to know very well what Christianity is, and he is prepared to educate the reader in dogmatic Christian concepts and to point out the ethical and religious inadequacies of philosophical idealism. Climacus will lead the reader to an understanding of what it means to be Christian, he will show that it requires a leap of faith that cannot be mediated in the categories of pure thought, while at the same time confessing that he is unable to make this leap. Thus Kierkegaard writes: "If it is an illusion that all are Christians— and if there is anything to be done about it, it must be done indirectly, not by one who vociferously proclaims himself an extraordinary Christian, but by one who, better instructed, is ready to declare that he is not a Christian at all."[58] By delivering the philosophical point within the indirect communication, Kierkegaard is at once able to preserve the indirection of the authorship and accomplish the religious purpose of exposing the illusion of Christendom.

Concluding Remarks

By way of concluding, I want to suggest that Kierkegaard's analysis of reason, faith, and revelation may provide an insightful way to resolve a long-standing territorial dispute between philosophers and theologians.

Traditionally, theologians have maintained that revelation cannot be understood from any standpoint external to faith. Representing an influential perspective within modern Protestant theology, Karl Barth writes:

> According to Holy Scripture God's revelation is a ground which has no sort of higher or deeper ground above or behind it, but is simply a ground in itself, and therefore as regards man an authority from which no appeal to a higher authority is possible. Its reality and likewise its truth do not rest upon a superior reality and truth, are under no need of an initial actualization or legitimation as a reality from any other such point, are not to be compared with such, nor to be judged and regarded as reality and truth in the light of such. . . . Obviously the adoption of revelation from the point of view of such a ground differing from it and presumably superior to it . . . can only be achieved by denying revelation. Revelation is not real and true from the standpoint of anything else, whether in itself or for us. It is so in itself, and for us through itself.[1]

For Barth, to be committed to the Christian doctrinal frame is to be committed to the claim that there is no human perspective higher than or superior to revelation according to which the latter can be judged. It follows that to seek an evidentially grounded confirmation of the truth of revelation is incompatible with the requirements of faith. Reason has no decisive bearing on the question of whether or not revelation is true.

From the philosopher's point of view, the picture described by Barth is rationally unacceptable. For what he says, in effect, is that the philosophical inquiry into the truth of revelation carries no weight in the theological realm. Speaking in behalf of the philosophers, Brand Blanshard explains:

> They would no doubt admit that in dealing with such dark problems as the nature of Deity and the origin and destiny of the world, reason halts and stumbles, but they would agree that if such things are to be known at all, they must be known by rational reflection which starts from the facts of experience and goes on to draw inferences from them; there is no quick non-rational road which, somehow skirting the infirmities of our natural powers and knowledge, conducts us to absolute truth.[2]

Nevertheless, philosophy cannot simply declare that the mysteries of Christian faith are a product of irrational superstition, for this would merely beg the question against Barth, who maintains that reason is in some sense inadequate as a judge of divine revelation. This does not mean that the philosopher is without recourse. But the manner in which he engages the theologian will depend on how the limits of reason are to be construed:

> If it means merely that reason as now exercised falls short of ultimate truth, we can only agree. If it means that the conflicts between revealed and natural insights are such as may be removed by expanding knowledge and are only a temporary veil for a coherent world beyond them, the question is on which side the revision is to take place. That revealed knowledge can be revised Barth would of course deny. What must be given up as it stands is therefore natural knowledge. But . . . the required revision of natural knowledge would revise it out of existence by denying the truth of insights that are clear and crucial. (299)

Barth is commonly interpreted as claiming that divine revelation calls for the unconditional surrender of human reason. On this antirationalist view, even if revelation demands that we abandon the law of contradiction itself, "it is ours not to reason why, but to obey" (299). But Blanshard argues that such a position is self-refuting:

Barth plainly expects us to accept his statements as true, his exposition as relevant, and his conclusions as valid. He expects us to accept all this while accepting at the same time his indictment of reason as unreliable, while believing that some of its clearest and most certain insights are false, while questioning even its simplest and most universal demands. (300–301)

If Barth claims that the laws of logic do not apply to revelation, then they cannot be appealed to in support of his own argument: either the laws of logic are universally valid, or else they are not valid at all. This antirationalist interpretation is not one that Barthians would readily accept. They would point out that Barth acknowledges the validity of reason within its proper sphere. What he insists on is the subordination of reason to the Word of God. Accordingly, it has been suggested that Barth's position might be characterized more accurately as 'nonrationalist'. But this still leaves him open to criticism. For the claim that reason has limits is certainly a claim that can be rationally examined, and therefore requires rational justification. The appeal to nonrationalism is ultimately neither accurate nor satisfactory.

It is here, however, that Kierkegaard may provide some insight. Without retreating to an antirationalist position, he shows that it is quite possible to distinguish between that which is a possible object for human knowledge and that which is not. There is no inconsistency in using reason to define its own limits. In fact, this assumption is central to Kierkegaard's analysis of revelation. On the one hand, he shows that there are logical reasons why the truth of Christian revelation cannot be a possible object for human knowledge. Yet he also recognizes that there must be some rational procedure for distinguishing between genuine and spurious claims to revelation. To see how Kierkegaard reconciles these views, we must recall two main features of his analysis.

As we saw in chapter 6, Kierkegaard draws our attention to the special function of Christian doctrine in regulating the speech and action of the believer. Christian doctrine creates an objective framework within which the believer is able to construct a coherent and intelligible understanding of self and world. The religious value of doctrinal statements can be seen in the fact that they are vehicles for being related to divine reality. Religious doctrines do not purport to be falsifiable descriptions of what divine reality is like, but rather specify how it is possible to participate in that reality. The New Testament narratives concerning the life, teaching, death, and resurrection of Jesus Christ form the basis of a comprehensive conceptual scheme, which not only shapes the subjectivity of the believer, but also serves as an objective standard for determining what constitutes faithful adherence to the Christian community.

The foregoing account of religious doctrine is supported by Kierkegaard's analysis of the logic of Christian revelation. Although the God of Christianity is a God of love, Kierkegaard stresses the essential mystery in God's revelation of that love. To the understanding, the God-man of the incarnation is the absolute paradox. Contrary to the Hegelian view, divine revelation transcends human knowledge and understanding. However, revelation does not destroy reason. Rather, it requires that the individual acknowledge the limits of reason and accept revelation as pointing the way to a higher truth. But as a condition for realizing this saving truth, revelation requires that the individual undergo a personal transformation. Repentance begins with a free act of will in which the individual renounces the claim to self-mastery and self-sufficiency, accepts the truth of divine revelation, and embraces Christ as his savior, thereby committing himself to a life of striving to imitate the ideal pattern.

Even though the decision to accept the Christ-revelation cannot be decided on theoretical grounds, it does not follow that the decision to believe (to become a disciple) is therefore groundless. For as we have seen, the absolute paradox reveals a basic tension within the concept of rationality itself. Whereas purely evidential considerations do not warrant the decision to believe, there are important practical and ethical considerations that may render that decision perfectly rational. Nor does it follow that there is no place for sustained philosophical reflection on the Christian form of life, or that claims to revelation cannot be subjected to rational examination. In his book on Adler, Kierkegaard specifically acknowledges the need for philosophical analysis to determine the conditions under which it is permissible to assert that something counts as a revelation in the Christian sense. Even if it is finally impossible to say whether a person has in fact received a divine revelation, it is possible to determine whether a person's statements and actions are consistent with such a claim.

In this way, Kierkegaard is able to do justice to the concerns of the theologian as well as the philosopher. He shows that the theologian is correct in maintaining that Christian revelation presents itself as a judgment upon human standards. But even though we are not in a position to judge revelation, we can and must be able to determine the conditions under which the term *revelation* has a coherent use in the Christian context; how the doctrine of revelation functions as a regulative principle for the Christian form of life. Kierkegaard's work in elucidating dogmatic Christian concepts is not only a paradigm of philosophical analysis, it demonstrates the possibility of finding common ground between philosophy and theology.

Bibliographical Note and Abbreviations

All quotations from the published works of Kierkegaard are taken from the standard English translations listed in the Bibliography, unless otherwise noted. Page references are followed in parentheses by the volume and page number of the corresponding Danish text. I have used the first edition of *Søren Kierkegaards Samlede Værker*, 14 vols., edited by A. B. Drachman, J. L. Heiberg, and H. O. Lange (Copenhagen: Gyldendals, 1901–1906). References to Kierkegaard's private papers are taken from *Søren Kierkegaard's Journals and Papers*, edited and translated by Howard V. Hong and Edna H. Hong (Bloomington, IN: Indiana University Press, 1967–1978). Each reference is followed in parentheses by the volume, section, and number of the corresponding Danish entry, as it appears in the second enlarged edition of *Søren Kierkegaards Papirer*, 13 vols., edited by P. A. Heiberg, Victor Kuhr, Einer Torsting, and Niels Thulstrup (Copenhagen: Gyldendals, 1968–1978). References to untranslated sections of the *Papirer* will cite only the Danish edition.

The following abbreviations are used for Kierkegaard's works:

A	*Two Ages: A Literary Review*
AN	*Armed Neutrality and An Open Letter*
CA	*The Concept of Anxiety*
COR	*The Corsair Affair*
CUP	*Concluding Unscientific Postscript*
EO	*Either/Or*
OAR	*On Authority and Revelation*
PC	*Practice in Christianity*
PF	*Philosophical Fragments*
PV	*The Point of View for My Work as an Author*
SKJP	*Søren Kierkegaard's Journals and Papers*
SUD	*The Sickness Unto Death*
SV	*Søren Kierkegaard's Samlede Værker*

Notes

INTRODUCTION

1. This view can be found, for example, in Walter Lowrie, *Kierkegaard*, vol. 2 (New York: Harper & Brothers, 1962), pp. 382–386, and more recently in Bruce Kirmmse, *Kierkegaard in Golden Age Denmark* (Bloomington and Indianapolis: Indiana University Press, 1990), p. 336.

CHAPTER 1. REVELATIONS OF SELF IN THE PSEUDONYMOUS AUTHORSHIP

1. The new Princeton translations prefer "upbuilding" to "edification." For a complete explanation of this point see Søren Kierkegaard, *Eighteen Upbuilding Discourses*, edited and translated by Howard V. Hong and Edna H. Hong (Princeton: Princeton University Press, 1990), pp. 503–505.

2. *Fædrelandet* no. 1162, February 27, 1843. This article is contained in *COR*, pp. 13–16 (*SV* XIII, pp. 407–410).

3. *CUP*, p. 551 (*SV* VII, p. 546).

4. Bertel Pedersen, "Fictionality and Authority: A Point of View for Kierkegaard's Work as an Author," in Harold Bloom (ed.) *Kierkegaard* (New York and Philadelphia: Chelsea House Publishers, 1989), p.104.

5. Some of the more influential representatives of this approach are Eduard Geismar, Theodor Hæcker, and Walter Lowrie.

6. C. Stephen Evans, *Kierkegaard's "Fragments" and "Postscript": The Religious Philosophy of Johannes Climacus* (Atlantic Highlands, NJ: Humanities Press, 1983), pp. 8–9.

7. This point is made by Kierkegaard in *PV*, p. 6 (*SV* XIII, p. 518).

8. Ibid., p. 5f. (*SV* XIII, p. 517f.).

9. Ibid., p. 103 (*SV* XIII, p. 582).

10. Ibid., p. 17f. (*SV* XIII, p. 525f.).

11. Ibid., p. 24 (*SV* XIII, p. 531).

12. Ibid., p. 26f. (*SV* XIII, p. 532f.).

13. Ibid., p. 39 (*SV* XIII, p. 540f.).

14. Ibid., p. 40f. (*SV* XIII, p. 541).

15. Paul L. Holmer, "Kierkegaard and Logic," *Kierkegaardiana* 2 (1957): 31.

16. Evans, p. 8.

17. Henning Fenger, *Kierkegaard, the Myths and Their Origins*, translated by George C. Schoolfield (New Haven and London: Yale University Press, 1980). The original Danish version of this book was published in 1976 by Odense Universitetsforlag under the title *Kierkegaard Myter og Kierkegaard Kilder.*

18. Alexander Nehamas, *Nietzsche: Life as Literature* (Cambridge and London: Harvard University Press, 1985), p. 3.

19. Fenger, p. 26.

20. Ibid., p. 147.

21. *PV*, p. 150 (*SV* XIII, p. 500).

22. George J. Stack, *International Studies in Philosophy* 15 (1983): 80.

23. These include two scholarly efforts: *From the Papers of One Still Living* (1838) and his dissertation *The Concept of Irony* (1841).

24. Fenger, p. 28.

25. Namely, "Who Is the Author of *Either/Or?* "

26. *COR*, p. 16 (*SV* XIII, p. 410).

27. *CUP*, p. 225 (*SV* VII, p. 212).

28. *CUP* (*SV* VII).

29. *PV*, p. 151 (*SV* XIII, p. 501).

30. Ibid., p. 15 (*SV* XIII, p. 524).

31. Ibid.

32. Ibid., p. 16 (*SV* XIII, p. 524).

33. Most notably Mark C. Taylor, Louis Mackey, and John D. Caputo.

34. Jonathan Culler, *On Deconstruction* (Ithaca: Cornell University Press, 1982), p. 94.

35. Jacques Derrida, *Of Grammatology*, translated by Gayatri Chakravorty Spivak (Baltimore and London: The Johns Hopkins University Press, 1974), p. 10ff.

36. Ibid.

37. W. V. O. Quine, *From a Logical Point of View* (Cambridge: Harvard University Press, 1953), p. 24.

38. Culler, p. 95.

39. Ibid., p. 96.

40. Jacques Derrida, *Positions*, translated and annotated by Alan Bass (Chicago and London: University of Chicago Press, 1981), p. 28.

41. Christopher Norris, *The Deconstructive Turn* (London and New York: Metheuen, 1983), p. 102.

42. Louis Mackey, "Points of View for His Work as an Author," In *Points of View: Readings of Kierkegaard* (Tallahassee: Florida State University Press, 1986), pp. 160–192.

43. Norris, p. 100.

44. Paul DeMan, *Allegories of Reading: Figural Languages in Rosseau, Nietzsche, Rilke and Proust* (New Haven and London: Yale University Press, 1979), p. 298; in Norris, p. 88.

45. *PV*, p. 40 (*SV* XIII, p. 541).

46. Cf. *SKJP*, vol. 1, pp. 649–657 (VIII^2 B 81–89).

47. *CUP* (*SV* VII).

48. Friederich Nietzsche, *Beyond Good and Evil*, trans. Walter Kaufmann (New York: Vintage Books, 1966), p. 47.

49. Ibid., 161.

50. *PV*, p. 16 (*SV* XIII, p. 525).

51. Norris, p. 89.

52. George Steiner, *Real Presences* (Chicago: University of Chicago Press, 1989), p. 229.

53. Norris, p. 90.

54. *PC*, p. 133 (*SV* XII, p. 124).

55. *PV*, pp. 144–146 (*SV* XIII, pp. 495–497).

56. *A*, p. 99 (*SV* VIII, p. 92).

57. Wayne C. Booth, *The Rhetoric of Fiction* (Chicago and London: The University of Chicago Press, 1961), p. 74.

58. Steiner, p. 214.

CHAPTER 2. KIERKEGAARD AS CHRISTIAN PHILOSOPHER

1. *PV,* pp. 5–6 (*SV* XIII, pp. 517–518).

2. *AN,* p. 35 (X⁵ B 107, pp. 289–290).

3. Ibid., p. 34 (X⁵ B 107, pp. 288–289).

4. *OAR,* p. 166 (VII² B 235, p. 201).

5. Immanuel Kant, *Critique of Pure Reason,* translated by Norman Kemp Smith (New York: St. Martin's Press, 1965), p. 653 (A832/B860).

6. G. W. F. Hegel, *Logic,* translated by William Wallace (New York: Oxford University Press, 1975), pp. 20–21 (§§14–16).

7. Hegel, *Lectures on the Philosophy of Religion,* 3 vols., translated by E.B. Speirs and J. Burdon Sanderson (New York: Humanities Press, 1962).

8. Quentin Lauer, "Hegel on the Identity of Content in Religion and Philosophy," in *Hegel and the Philosophy of Religion,* edited by Darrel E. Christensen (The Hague: Martinus Nijhoff, 1970), p. 271.

9. Hegel, *Lectures on the Philosophy of Religion,* vol. 1, p. 206.

10. Hermann Diem, *Kierkegaard: An Introduction,* translated by David Green (Richmond: John Knox Press, 1966), pp. 71–80.

11. C. F. Wolff, *Vernünftige Gedanken von Gott, der Welt und der Seele, auch allen Dingen überhaupt* (1719), par. 29; quoted from Michael Inwood, *A Hegel Dictionary* (Cambridge: Blackwell Publishers, 1992), p. 10. See *PF,* p. 75 (*SV* IV, p. 339).

12. *PF,* p. 73 (*SV* IV, p. 263–264). Cf. W.G. Tennemann, *Geschichte der Philosophie,* 11 vols. (Leipzig, 1798–1819), see vol. 3, esp. pp. 125–127. *SKJP,* vol. 1, pp. 109–110 (IV C 47–48, 80).

13. Ibid., p. 75 (*SV* IV, p. 239).

14. *CUP,* pp. 100, 267n. (*SV* VII, pp. 89, 258n.). See Adolph Trendelenburg's *Logische Untersuchungen* 2 vols. (Berlin, 1840) and *Die logische Frage in Hegels System* (Leipzig, 1843). Thulstrup surmises that Kierkegaard's reading of Trendelenburg began in earnest in March of 1844, citing *SKJP* vol. 3, pp. 16, 514 (V A 74, 98). See Niels Thulstrup, *Commentary on Kierkegaard's Concluding Unscientific Postscript,* translated by Robert J. Widenmann (Princeton: Princeton University Press, 1984), p. 224.

15. *CUP,* pp. 101–102 (*SV* VII, p. 91).

16. Ibid., p. 103 (*SV* VII, p. 92). Cf. *SKJP,* vol. 3, pp. 717–718 (X¹ A 66).

17. Ibid.

18. Ibid., p. 104 (*SV* VII, p. 93).

19. Ibid., p. 107 (*SV* VII, p. 97).

20. Ibid., p. 109 (*SV* VII, p. 99). As Stephen Crites notes, Kierkegaard's point "is not so much that Hegel's interpretation of individuality was deficient (though he did think it was), but rather that the system itself, in virtue of its direct, discursive presentation of truth as a totality, was a form of thinking inherently alien to the individual's situation in existence, that indeed it manifested a comic 'absent-mindedness' in the philosopher about the way he himself is situated in existence." *In the Twilight of Christendom: Hegel vs. Kierkegaard on Faith and History,* AAR Studies in Religion, edited by W.G. Oxtoby (Chambersburg, PA: American Academy of Religion, 1972), p. 28.

21. Inwood, p. 266.

22. *CUP*, p. 109 (*SV* VII, p. 98).

23. *SUD*, p. 13 (*SV* XI, p. 127). In *The Concept of Anxiety,* it is characterized more simply as a synthesis of body and soul (psyche) which is grounded in spirit. See *CA*, pp. 48, 85 (*SV* IV, pp. 319, 355).

24. *SUD*, p. 29 (*SV* XI, p. 142).

25. James Collins, *The Mind of Kierkegaard* (Princeton: Princeton University Press, 1983), p. 205.

26. *SUD*, p. 29 (*SV* XI, p. 142).

27. *EO*, vol. 2, pp. 223–224, 250–251 (*SV* II, pp. 200, 225–226).

28. *CUP*, pp. 306–307 (*SV* VII, p. 297).

29. John D. Caputo, *Radical Hermeneutics: Repetition, Deconstruction, and the Hermeneutic Project* (Bloomington and Indianapolis: University of Indiana Press, 1987), p. 18.

30. Ibid., p. 21. Cf. *Papirer,* IV B 177.

31. *CUP*, pp. 273–274. (*SV* VII, p. 264–265).

32. Ibid., p. 506 (*SV* VII, p. 497).

33. *SKJP*, vol. 1, p. 450 (IV A 164).

34. Niels Thulstrup, *Kierkegaards forhold til Hegel og til den spekulative Idealisme indtil 1846* (Copenhagen: Gyldendal, 1967), p. 101. The same point is made by James Collins, who notes that Kierkegaard "had earlier and wider acquaintance with the mass of Hegelian and anti-Hegelian writings, which followed close upon the master's death, than with the actual text of Hegel himself" (Collins, p. 104).

35. Kierkegaard was also in Berlin between 1841 and 1842, where he attended lectures by the Hegelian theologian Philip Marheineke, F. W. J. Schelling, and Karl Werder. Werder's lectures were subsequently published as *Logik als Commentar und Ergänzung zu Hegels Wissenschaft der Logik* (Berlin, 1841).

36. Thulstrup (pp. 133–135) gives a brief synopsis of the main critical points of Sibbern's essay.

37. *PF*, pp. 108–109 (*SV* IV, p. 270).

38. Mark C. Taylor, *Journeys to Selfhood: Hegel and Kierkegaard* (Berkeley and Los Angeles: University of California Press, 1980), p. 166.

39. Taylor, pp. 147–148.

40. *SKJP*, vol. 1, p. 329 (IV A 192). The translator notes that the reference is probably to Hegel's *Vorlesungen über die Geschichte der Philosophie* (Berlin, 1833), vol. 1, pp. 32 and 37.

41. *CUP*, pp. 270–271 (*SV* VII, p. 261). Cf. *CUP*, p. 310 (*SV* VII, p. 301).

42. Ibid., p. 270 (*SV* VII, p. 261).

43. Ibid., p. 296 (*SV* VII, p. 287).

44. Ibid., pp. 199–200 (*SV* VII, pp. 186–187).

45. Ibid., p. 271 (*SV* VII, pp. 261–262).

46. *A*, p. 97 (*SV* VIII, p. 90).

47. J. N. Findlay, "Reflexive Asymmetry: Hegel's Most Fundamental Methodological Ruse," in *Beyond Epistemology: New Studies in the Philosophy of Hegel*, edited by F. G. Weiss (The Hague: Martinus Nijhoff, 1974), p. 162. This view is favored by Taylor, p. 148n.

48. Collins, p. 105.

49. *CUP*, p. 270, (*SV* VII, p. 261).

50. Holmer, p. 26.

51. *CUP*, p. 291 (*SV* VII, p. 282).

52. Ibid., p. 262 (*SV* VII, p. 253).

53. *SKJP*, vol. 2, pp. 217–220 (V B 41).

54. *CUP*, p. 359 (*SV* VII, p. 348).

55. See *CA*, p. 28 (*SV* IV, p. 300). See also p. 29 (*SV* IV, p. 301).

56. *SUD*, p. 120 (*SV* XI, p. 230).

57. Ibid., p. 119 (*SV* XI, p. 228).

58. Ibid., p. 120 (*SV* XI, p. 230).

59. *SKJP*, vol. 2, p. 282 (X^1 A 646).

60. *PV*, p. 37 (*SV* XIII, p. 539).

61. *OAR*, p. xv (VIII² B 27, p. 75).

62. *AN*, p. 34 (X⁵ B 107, pp. 288–289).

63. Ibid., pp. 34–35 (X⁵ B 107, p. 290).

64. See, for example, *CUP*, p. 178ff. (*SV* VII, p. 166ff.).

65. *OAR*, p. xvi (VIII² B 27, p. 26).

66. Ibid., p. 167 (VII² B 235, p. 204).

67. Ibid., p. 165 (VII² B 235, p. 202).

68. *SKJP*, vol. 3, pp. 365–366 (VIII² B 15).

69. Stanley Cavell, "Kierkegaard's *On Authority and Revelation*," in *Must We Mean What We Say?* (New York: Cambridge University Press, 1976), p. 168.

70. *SKJP*, vol. 3, pp. 496–497 (I A 94).

71. *CUP*, p. 101 (*SV* VII, p. 90).

72. Ibid., p. 279 (*SV* VII, p. 270).

73. *SKJP*, vol. 3, p. 521 (X² A 432). In the *Postscript*, Kierkegaard writes: "Dialectics itself does not see the absolute, but it leads, as it were, the individual up to it, and says: 'Here it must be, that I guarantee; when you worship here, you worship God.' But worship itself is not dialectics. A dialectic that mediates is a derelict genius," pp. 438–439 (*SV* VII, pp. 426–427).

74. Ibid., vol. 3, p. 500 (II A 77).

CHAPTER 3. REASON, FAITH, AND REVELATION

1. Cf. Torsten Bohlin, *Kierkegaards Tro och Andra Kierkegaard Studier* (Stockholm: Svenska Kyrkans Diakonistyrelsens Bokförlag, 1944); William Barrett, *Irrational Man* (Garden City: Doubleday, 1962); A. E. Murphy, "On Kierkegaard's Claim that 'Truth is Subjectivity,'" in *Reason and the Common Good* (Englewood Cliffs: Prentice Hall, 1963); Herbert M. Garelick, *The Anti-Christianity of Kierkegaard* (The Hague: Martinus Nijhoff, 1965); Brand Blanshard, "Kierkegaard on Faith," *Personalist* 49 (1968); Louis P. Pojman, *The Logic of Subjectivity* (University: University of Alabama Press, 1984).

2. Pojman, p. 141.

3. *CUP*, p. 188 (*SV* VII, p. 176).

4. Ibid., pp. 208–209 (*SV* VII, pp. 196).

5. Ibid., pp. 206 (*SV* VII, pp. 193).

6. A similar case is made by Pojman, pp. 87–117.

7. David Hume, *A Treatise of Human Nature,* edited by L.A. Selby Bigge, second edition revised by P.H. Nidditch (London: Oxford University Press, 1978), p. 624.

8. Richard Swinburne, *Faith and Reason* (New York: Oxford University Press, 1981), p. 25.

9. Swinburne defines a basic proposition as a proposition which seems to S to be true, not because it is made probable by other propositions S accepts, but because S is inclined to believe that it is forced on him by his experience of the world.

10. Blanshard, "Kierkegaard on Faith," p. 14.

11. Ibid., p. 15.

12. I do not mean to claim that Kierkegaard sees faith primarily as a form of intellectual assent to doctrinal propositions. I am merely observing that Christianity demands adherence to its doctrines, and that this aspect of faith, whether or not it is secondary to the fiducial aspect (and for Kierkegaard I think it clearly is), must be accounted for. It must not be forgotten that Kierkegaard's Christian pseudonym, Anti-Climacus, has no problem affirming his belief in the doctrines of Christianity.

13. Blanshard, pp. 15–16.

14. *CUP,* p. 504 (*SV* VII, p. 495).

15. *SKJP,* vol. 1, p. 5 (X^2 A 354).

16. *Philosophical Fragments,* trans. David F. Swenson with revisions by Howard V. Hong (Princeton: Princeton University Press, 1967), pp. 136–137 (*SV* IV, p. 270).

17. Cf. *SKJP,* vol. 1, p. 11 (X^5 A 120); p. 61 (VIII^1 A 88); p. 329 (IV A 57); p. 329 (V A 68); vol. 3, p. 274 (VII^1 A 191); *PF,* pp. 86–88 (*SV* IV, pp. 249–251); *CUP,* pp. 32, 188 (*SV* VII, pp. 20, 176). A similar argument is made by C. Stephen Evans in "Is Kierkegaard an Irrationalist? Reason, Paradox, and Faith," *Religious Studies* 25 (1989): 347–362.

18. Cf. *SKJP,* vol. 3, p. 400 (IV A 47); pp. 402–403 (V B 5:10); p. 406 (VIII^1 A 273); pp. 410–411 (X^5 A 142); *PF,* pp. 37–39 (*SV* IV, pp. 204–207); *CUP,* p. 201 (*SV* VII, p. 188).

19. *SKJP,* vol. 3, p. 402 (IV B 75).

20. *CUP,* pp. 194–198 (*SV* VII, pp. 181–185).

21. Ibid., pp. 191–192 (*SV* VII, pp. 179–180).

22. *SKJP,* vol. 1, p. 4 (X^2 A 354).

23. Ibid., vol. 1, p. 7 (X^2 B 79).

24. Ibid., vol. 1, p. 4 (X^2 A 354).

25. Henry Allison, "Christianity and Nonsense," *Review of Metaphysics* 20 (1967): 432.

26. J. Heywood Thomas, *Subjectivity and Paradox* (Oxford: Basil Blackwell, 1957), p. 133.

27. *SKJP*, vol. 1, p. 8 (X^6 B 80).

28. Ibid., vol. 1, p. 5 (X^2 A 354).

29. Ibid., vol. 1, p. 7 (X^6 B 79).

30. Ibid., vol. 1, p. 5 (X^2 A 354).

31. Ibid., vol. 3, p. 365 (VIII^2 B 15).

32. Ibid., vol. 3, pp. 399–400 (IV C 29).

33. Cf. N. H. Søe, "Kierkegaard's Doctrine of the Paradox," and Cornelio Fabro, "Faith and Reason in Kierkegaard's Dialectic," in *A Kierkegaard Critique*, ed. Howard Johnson and Niels Thulstrup (New York: Harper & Row, 1962).

34. Pojman, *The Logic of Subjectivity*, p. 131.

35. Niels Thulstrup, introduction to *Philosophical Fragments*, by Søren Kierkegaard, trans. David F. Swenson with revisions by Howard V. Hong (Princeton: Princeton University Press, 1967), p. lxix.

36. *PF*, p. 17 (*SV* IV, p. 187).

37. Ibid., p. 37 (*SV* IV, p. 204).

38. Ibid.

39. Ibid., p. 39 (*SV* IV, p. 206).

40. Ibid., p. 39 (*SV* IV, p. 207).

41. Ibid., p. 44 (*SV* IV, p. 212).

42. *SKJP*, vol. 4, pp. 213–214 (X^3 A 235).

43. *PF*, pp. 46–47 (*SV* IV, p. 214).

44. Ibid., pp. 45–46 (*SV* IV, p. 213).

45. Ibid., p. 45 (*SV* IV, p. 212).

46. Ibid., p. 45 (*SV* IV, p. 213).

47. Ibid., p. 47 (*SV* IV, p. 214).

48. Ibid., p. 47 (*SV* IV, p. 214).

49. *SKJP*, vol. 3, p. 400 (IV C 84, A 47).

50. *PF*, p. 101 (*SV* IV, pp. 263–264).

51. *Philosophical Fragments,* trans. David F. Swenson with revisions by Howard V. Hong (Princeton, NJ: Princeton University Press, 1967), p. 222.

52. Gordon D. Kaufman, "Philosophy of Religion and Christian Theology," *Journal of Religion* 37 (1957): 238.

53. *PF*, p. 51 (*SV* IV, p. 217).

54. *OAR*, p. 58 (VII² B 235, pp. 75–76).

55. Ibid., p. 49 (*SV* IV, pp. 215–216).

56. *SKJP*, vol 2, p. 321 (X¹ A 455).

57. Matthew 16: 25–26 RSV. Cf. Luke 14: 28–33 RSV.

58. *CUP*, pp. 20, 28, 33 (*SV* VII, pp. 7–8, 16, 21).

59. Ibid., pp. 147–158 (*SV* IX, pp. 138–148).

60. For a detailed discussion of this point, see Jeremy Walker, "Ethical Beliefs: A Theory of Truth Without Truth-Values," *Thought* 218 (1980): 295–305.

61. *SKJP*, vol. 3, pp. 543–545 (X³ A 143).

62. *CUP*, p. 208 (*SV* VII, p. 195).

63. Ibid., pp. 208–209 (*SV* VII, p. 196).

64. Ibid., p. 209 (*SV* VII, p. 196).

65. *SKJP*, vol. 2, p. 320 (X¹ A 455).

66. Ibid.

67. William James, "The Will to Believe," in *The Works of William James: The Will to Believe* (Cambridge: Harvard University Press, 1979), pp. 13–33.

68. Ibid., p. 18. The quotation is taken from the second volume of Clifford's *Lectures and Essays,* ed. Leslie Stephen and Frederick Pollack, 2 vols. (London: Macmillan and Co., 1879), p. 183.

69. Ibid., p. 20.

70. "The Sentiment of Rationality," in *The Works of William James: The Will To Believe*, pp. 57–89.

71. James, "The Will to Believe," p. 14.

72. *PF*, p. 84 (*SV* IV, p. 248).

73. Ibid., pp. 82–83 (*SV* IV, pp. 246). Cf. James, "The Will to Believe," p. 30.

74. *PF*, p. 82 (*SV* IV, pp. 245–246).

75. Ibid., p. 84 (*SV* IV, p. 247).

76. Ibid., pp. 83 (*SV* IV, pp. 247).

77. James, "The Will to Believe," p. 28.

78. Ibid., p. 30.

79. *SKJP*, vol. 3, pp. 239–251 (VII[1] A 182–182, 186, 188–191, 194–200), pp. 252–254 (X[5] A 73); *CUP*, pp. 23–31 (*SV* VII, pp. 11–19).

80. James, "The Will to Believe," p. 26.

81. *SKJP*, vol. 4, p. 493 (X[1] A 410). Cf. p. 347 (VI A 64).

82. James, "The Will to Believe," p. 27.

83. *CUP*, pp. 147–148 (*SV* VII, p. 137).

84. Ibid., pp. 148–149 (*SV* VII, p. 137).

85. Ibid., p. 149 (*SV* VII, p. 138).

86. Ibid., p. 154 (*SV* VII, p. 143).

87. Ibid., p. 155–156 (*SV* VII, p. 144).

88. Ibid., p. 19 (*SV* VII, p. 7).

89. Ibid., p. 31 (*SV* VII, p. 19).

90. *SKJP*, vol. 3, p. 717 (X[1] A 66).

91. *CUP*, pp. 302–305 (*SV* VII, pp. 293–296).

92. *SKJP*, vol. 4, p. 118 (X[3] A 341).

93. *CUP*, p. 239 (*SV* VII, pp. 226–227).

94. Ibid., pp. 191–192 (*SV* VII, pp. 179–180).

95. Ibid., p. 190 (*SV* VII, p. 178).

96. *PF*, p. 14 (*SV* IV, p. 184).

97. *CUP*, p. 239 (*SV* VII, p. 227).

98. *PF*, p. 18 (*SV* IV, p. 188).

99. Ibid., p. 23 (*SV* VI, p. 23).

100. Ibid., p. 21 (*SV* VI, p. 21).

101. *SKJP*, vol. 1, p. 7 (X^6 B 79).

102. Ibid., vol. 1, p. 4 (X^2 A 354).

103. Ibid., vol. 2, p. 165 (X^2 A 198).

104. Ibid., vol. 2, p. 166 (X^2 A 223).

105. Ibid., vol. 3, pp. 409–410 (X^3 A 424).

106. *CUP*, pp. 182, 362 (*SV* VII, pp. 170–171, 351).

107. Ibid., p. 362 (*SV* VII, p. 351).

108. *SKJP*, vol. 5, p. 447 (VIII^1 A 650).

CHAPTER 4. REVELATION AND HISTORY

1. *PF*, p. 9 (*SV* IV, pp. 179–180). Cf. Plato, *Meno*, translated by W. R. M. Lamb (Cambridge: Harvard University Press, 1924), 80d.

2. *PF*, p. 11 (*SV* IV, p. 181).

3. Ibid., p. 15 (*SV* IV, p. 185).

4. Ibid., p. 18 (*SV* IV, p. 188).

5. Plato, *Symposium*, Translated by W. R. M. Lamb (Cambridge: Harvard University Press, 1925), p. 205.

6. Ibid.

7. George Mavrodes, *Revelation and Religious Belief* (Philadelphia: Temple University Press, 1988), p. 54.

8. *PF*, p. 18 (*SV* IV, p. 188).

9. Mark C. Taylor, *Kierkegaard's Pseudonymous Authorship: A Study of Time and the Self* (Princeton: Princeton University Press, 1975), pp. 291ff.

10. Paul Müller, *Meddelelsensdialektik i Søren Kierkegaards Philosophiske Smuler* (Copenhagen: C.A. Reitzels Boghandel, 1979), p. 41.

11. *PF*, p. 104 (*SV* IV, p. 266).

12. Ibid., pp. 100–102 (*SV* IV, pp. 263–264).

13. *CUP*, p. 25 (*SV* VII, p. 13).

14. Ibid., p. 27 (*SV* VII, p. 15).

15. Ibid.

16. Ibid., p. 29 (*SV* VII, p. 17).

17. Ibid., p. 41 (*SV* VII, p. 30).

18. Ibid., p. 511 (*SV* VII, pp. 502–503).

19. Ibid., p. 28 (*SV* VII, p. 16).

20. Ibid., p. 26 (*SV* VII, p. 13).

21. Ibid., p. 31 (*SV* VII, p. 19).

22. Ibid., p. 28 (*SV* VII, p. 16).

23. Ibid., p. 180 (*SV* VII, p. 168).

24. Ibid., p. 31 (*SV* VII, p. 19).

25. *PF*, p. 83 (*SV* IV, p. 247).

26. *CUP*, p. 180 (SV VII, p. 168). The reference here is to Socrates, but there can be no mistake that this is intended as a model for the Christian believer.

27. Kant, *Critique of Practical Reason*, Book II, Chap. 2, Secs. 4–5.

28. Kant, *Critique of Pure Reason*, B 857.

29. *PF*, p. 84 (*SV* IV, p. 247).

30. Ronald M. Green, *Kierkegaard and Kant: The Hidden Debt* (Albany: State University of New York Press, 1992), p. 176.

31. Kant, *The Conflict of the Faculties*, p. 63. Quoted in Green, p. 176.

32. Kant, p. 119.

33. Green, p. 176.

34. *SKJP*, vol. 1, p. 270 (VIII² B 81:10).

35. *PF*, p. 15 (*SV* IV, p. 185).

36. Ibid.

37. See, for example, the Supplement to *PF* (p. 187), where the following text appears: "That other teacher, then, must be God himself. As the occasion, he acts to remind me that I am untruth and am that through my own fault; as God, he also gives the condition with the truth," *Papirer,* V B 3:8.

38. *PF*, p. 99 (*SV* IV, p. 262).

39. Ibid.

40. See, for example, C. Stephen Evans, "The Relevance of Historical Evidence for Christian Faith: A Critique of a Kierkegaardian View," *Faith and Philosophy* 7 (1990): 470–484. This argument appears also in his recent book, *Passionate*

Reason: Making Sense of Kierkegaard's Philosophical Fragments (Bloomington: Indiana University Press, 1992), pp. 152–166.

41. Evans, "Relevance of Historical Evidence," p. 475.

42. The same point is made by Robert Merrihew Adams, who refers to this as the "Postponement Argument." See "Kierkegaard's Arguments Against Objective Reasoning in Religion," in *Contemporary Philosophy of Religion*, ed. S. Cahn and D. Shatz (New York and Oxford: Oxford University Press, 1982), pp. 218–221. This article originally appeared in *The Monist* 60 (1977): 228–243.

43. Evans, "Relevance of Historical Evidence," p. 478.

44. Ibid.

45. Ibid.

46. *PC,* p. 97 (*SV* XII, p. 93).

47. Evans, "Relevance of Historical Evidence," p. 470.

48. Ibid., p. 479.

49. John Stuart Mill, *Three Essays on Religion* (New York: Greenwood Press, 1969), p. 239.

50. Evans, "Relevance of Historical Evidence," pp. 470, 484.

51. Brand Blanshard, *Reason and Belief* (New Haven: Yale University Press, 1975), p. 219.

52. *PF,* pp. 50–51 (*SV* IV, p. 217).

53. Ibid., pp. 95–96 (*SV* IV, pp. 258–259).

54. Blaise Pascal, *Pensees,* translated by W. F. Trotter (London: J. M. Dent & Sons Ltd. and New York: E. P. Dutton & Co., Inc., 1943), p. 66.

55. Ibid.

56. *PF,* pp. 39–44 (*SV* IV, pp. 207–211). Knowledge is understood here in its objective, scientific sense. Kierkegaard agreed with Pascal's view that "knowledge of the divine is essentially a transformation of the person." *SKJP,* vol. 3, p. 420 (X³ A 609).

57. Neander, *Über die geschichtliche Bedeutung der pensees Pascals* (Berlin, 1847).

58. *SKJP,* vol. 3, p. 420 (X³ A 609).

59. Pascal, p. 67.

60. *CUP,* p. 179 (*SV* VII, p. 168).

61. Ibid., p. 512 (*SV* VII, p. 504).

62. Green, p. 134. Though my aim is not to demonstrate Kierkegaard's indebtedness to Kant in these matters, Green's excellent study amply supports the parallel I wish to draw. I am grateful for his insights in this section.

63. Ibid., p. 137.

64. Ibid., p. 136.

65. *CUP*, p. 179 (*SV* VII, p. 168).

66. Green, p. 139.

67. Ibid., p. 133.

68. Ibid., p. 143.

69. Ibid.

CHAPTER 5. GRACE AND WILL IN THE TRANSITION TO FAITH

1. *PF*, p. 62 (*SV* IV, p. 227).

2. See, for example, *SKJP*, vol. 2, pp. 163–164 (X A 507), *SKJP*, vol. 2, p. 169 (X^3 A 269), and *SKJP*, vol. 2, pp. 169–170 (X^3 A 353).

3. *PF*, p. 83ff (*SV* IV, p. 247f.).

4. *SKJP*, vol. 2, p. 3 (I A 36).

5. *PF*, pp. 47, 54, 59 (*SV* IV, pp. 215, 220, 224), *SKJP*, vol. 3, p. 404 (VI B 43), and *SKJP*, vol. 3, pp. 408–409 (X^2 A 501).

6. *PF*, pp. 43, 72–88 (*SV* IV, pp. 210, 235–251), *SKJP*, vol. 3, p. 19 (V C 7), *SKJP*, vol. 3, p. 20 (VI B 35:30), *SKJP*, vol. 3, p. 22 (VIII A 681), *SKJP*, vol. 3, p. 22 (X A 361), and *SKJP*, vol. 3, pp. 22–23 (XI^2 A 103).

7. David Wisdo, "Kierkegaard on Belief, Faith, and Explanation," *International Journal for Philosophy of Religion* 21:2 (1987): 110.

8. Pojman, *The Logic of Subjectivity*, pp. 103–107.

9. *Papirer*, V B 6:2.

10. *PF*, p. 59 (*SV* IV, p. 224).

11. George Stengren, "Faith," *Kierkegaardiana* 12 (1982): 81–92.

12. C. Stephen Evans, *Kierkegaard's "Fragments" and "Postscript": The Religious Philosophy of Johannes Climacus* (Atlantic Highlands, NJ: Humanities Press International, 1983), p. 268.

13. Pojman, p. 101.

14. Evans, p. 268.

15. Pojman, p. 101.

16. C. Stephen Evans, "Does Kierkegaard Think Beliefs Can be Directly Willed?", *International Journal for Philosophy of Religion* 26 (1989): 182.

17. M. Jamie Ferreira, *Transforming Vision: Imagination and Will in Kierke-gaardian Faith*, (Oxford: The Clarendon Press, 1991), p. 149.

18. Evans, *Kierkegaard's "Fragments" and "Postscript,"* p. 274.

19. Pojman, p. 21.

20. Karl Rahner, ed., *Encyclopedia of Theology, The Concise Sacramentum Mundi* (New York: Crossroads Publishing Co., 1982), p. 598.

21. *PF*, p. 49 (*SV* IV, p. 216).

22. Ibid., p. 50 (*SV* IV, p. 216f.).

23. *SKJP*, vol. 4, p. 352 (X^2 A 301).

24. Pojman, p. 91.

25. *PF*, p. 17 (*SV* IV, p. 187), and especially *SKJP*, vol. 2, p. 19 (X^3 A 323) and *SKJP*, vol. 2, p. 97 (VII A 139).

26. M. Jamie Ferreira, "Kierkegaardian Faith: 'the Condition' and the Response," *International Journal for Philosophy of Religion* 28 (1990): 63–79.

27. *PF*, pp. 14–15 (*SV* IV, p. 184).

28. Ibid., p. 18 (*SV* IV, p. 188).

29. Ibid., p. 19 (*SV* IV, p. 188).

30. Ferreira, "Kierkegaardian Faith," pp. 69–70.

31. *PF*, pp. 62–63 (*SV* IV, pp. 227–228).

32. Ibid., p. 14 (*SV* IV, p. 184).

33. Ferreira, "Kierkegaardian Faith," p. 73.

34. *PF*, p. 65 (*SV* IV, p. 229).

35. *PF*, p. 47 (*SV* IV, p. 215).

36. Ferreira, "Kierkegaardian Faith," pp. 75–76.

37. Ibid., p. 73.

38. M. Jamie Ferreira, *Transforming Vision: Imagination and Will in Kierke-gaardian Faith* (Oxford: The Clarendon Press, 1991).

39. Ibid., pp. 72–76.

40. Thomas Kuhn, *The Structure of Scientific Revolutions* (Chicago: University of Chicago Press, 1970), pp. 85.

41. Ibid., p. 150.

42. Ferreira, *Transforming Vision*, p. 35.

43. *PF*, pp. 18–19 (*SV* IV, pp. 188).

44. *CUP*, p. 573 (*SV* VII, p. 500).

45. *PF*, pp. 95–97 (*SV* IV, pp. 258–260).

46. *Concluding Unscientific Postscript*, 2 vols., ed. and trans. Howard V. Hong and Edna H. Hong (Princeton: Princeton University Press, 1992), p. 367n. (*SV* VII, pp. 318–319n.).

47. *PF*, p. 21 (*SV* IV, p. 190).

48. Ibid., p. 14 (*SV* IV, p. 184).

49. Ibid., pp. 18–19 (*SV* IV, p. 190).

50. *CUP*, p. 15 (*SV* VII, p. 3).

51. Ibid., p. 188 (*SV* VII, p. 176).

52. Ibid., p. 91 (*SV* VII, p. 79).

53. Ibid., p. 343 (*SV* VII, p. 333).

54. Ibid.

55. Robert C. Solomon, *About Love: Reinventing Romance for Our Times* (New York: Touchstone Books, 1988), p. 43. Solomon restates this position in a more recent work entitled *Love: Emotion, Myth and Metaphor* (New York: Prometheus Books, 1990). See especially the Preface and pp. 48–50, 216–227. The following references are to this work, unless otherwise noted.

56. Solomon, *About Love*, p. 126.

57. Ferreira, *Transforming Vision*, p. 120.

58. Ibid., p. 121.

59. Samuel Taylor Coleridge, *Biographia Literaria* (London: J. M. Dent and Sons Ltd., 1949), p. 60.

60. *SKJP*, vol. 3, p. 18 (V C 6).

61. William James, *Principles of Psychology*, vol. 2 (New York: Dover Publishers, 1950), p. 525.

62. Ibid.

63. Ferreira, *Transforming Vision,* p. 103.

64. James, p. 561.

65. Ferreira, *Transforming Vision,* p. 102.

66. James, p. 534.

67. *CUP,* p. 304 (*SV* VII, p. 295).

68. Ibid., p. 182 (*SV* VII, pp. 170–171).

69. *SKJP,* vol. 3, p. 18 (V C 6).

70. *CUP,* p. 192 (*SV* VII, p. 180).

71. *SKJP,* vol. 1, p. 92 (IX A 32).

72. *CUP,* p. 182 (*SV* VII, p. 170).

73. *SKJP,* vol. 6, p. 576 (XI^2 A 439).

CHAPTER 6. SUBJECTIVITY, TRUTH, AND DOCTRINE

1. George Lindbeck, *The Nature of Doctrine: Religion and Theology in a Postliberal Age* (Philadelphia: The Westminster Press, 1984).

2. I owe this point to Lee C. Barrett, "Theology as Grammar: Regulative Principles or Paradigms and Practices," *Modern Theology* 4 (1988): 156.

3. Lindbeck, p. 68.

4. J. L. Austin, "Performative Utterances," in *Philosophical Papers* (Oxford: Clarendon Press, 1970).

5. Lindbeck, p. 65.

6. Ludwig Wittgenstein, *Lectures and Conversations on Aesthetics, Psychology, and Religious Belief* (Berkeley: University of California Press, 1983), p. 57.

7. Ludwig Wittgenstein, *Culture and Value,* translated by Peter Winch (Chicago: University of Chicago Press, 1980), p. 33e.

8. Lindbeck, pp. 119–120.

9. Wittgenstein, *Culture and Value,* p. 29e.

10. Lindbeck, p. 33.

11. Wittgenstein, *Culture and Value,* p. 53e.

12. Lindbeck, p. 120.

13. *CUP*, p. 331 (*SV* VII, p. 321).

14. Ibid., p. 332 (*SV* VII, p. 321).

15. Ibid., p. 19 (*SV* VII, p. 8).

16. Ibid., p. 537 (*SV* VII, p. 529).

17. Ibid., p. 29 (*SV* VII, p. 17).

18. Ibid., p. 27 (*SV* VII, p. 15).

19. Ibid.

20. Ibid., p. 25 (*SV* VII, p. 12).

21. Ibid., p. 30 (*SV* VII, p. 18).

22. Ibid., p. 31 (*SV* VII, p. 19). Cf. Wittgenstein's remark: "The historical accounts in the Gospels might, historically speaking, be demonstrably false and yet belief would lose nothing by this . . . because historical proof (the historical proof-game) is irrelevant to belief" (*Culture and Value*, p. 32e.).

23. Ibid., p. 37 (*SV* VII, p. 26).

24. Ibid., p. 178 (*SV* VII, p. 199).

25. Ibid., p. 193 (*SV* VII, p. 180).

26. Ibid., p. 339n. (*SV* VII, pp. 328–329).

27. Ibid., p. 193 (*SV* VII, pp. 180–181).

28. Ibid., p. 184 (*SV* VII, p. 172).

29. Wittgenstein, *Culture and Value*, p. 32e.

30. *PF*, pp. 87–88 (*SV* IV, pp. 250–251).

31. Wittgenstein, *Lectures and Conversations*, p. 57.

32. *CUP*, p. 189 (*SV* VII, p. 177).

33. *SKJP*, vol. 1, p. 107 (IX A 32).

34. *PC*, pp. 204–205 (*SV* XII, pp. 188–189).

35. *CUP*, p. 116 (*SV* VII, p. 105).

36. *Papirer*, X^2 A 299.

37. See, for example, Pojman, *The Logic of Subjectivity*, pp. 70–71.

38. *CUP*, p. 70n. (*SV* VII, p. 59n.).

39. *PC*, pp. 205–206 (*SV* XII, p. 189). Cf. *CUP*, p. 201 (*SV* VII, p. 188).

40. Lindbeck, *The Nature of Doctrine*, p. 51.

41. *SKJP*, vol. 2, p. 97 (VII¹ A 139).

42. Immanuel Kant, *Critique of Pure Reason* (New York: St. Martin's Press, 1965), pp. 595–596.

43. Cf. John Hick's use of the Kantian model in *Philosophy of Religion* (Englewood Cliffs: Prentice-Hall, 1983), pp. 118–121.

44. *SKJP*, vol. 1, p. 240 (X¹ A 537). Cf. *Papirer*, X⁴ A 204.

45. Crites, *In the Twilight of Christendom*, p. 59.

46. *Kierkegaard's Attack Upon "Christendom,"* trans. Walter Lowrie with a supplementary introduction by Howard A. Johnson (Princeton: Princeton University Press, 1968), p. xxiii.

47. *Papirer*, X³ A 416.

48. Ronald L. Hall, *Word and Spirit: A Kierkegaardian Critique of the Modern Age* (Bloomington and Indianapolis: Indiana University Press, 1993), p. 202.

49. *OAR*, p. 163 (VII² B 235, p. 200).

50. *CA*, p. 95 (*SV* IV, p. 364).

51. Hall, p. 4.

52. Crites, p. 59.

53. *OAR*, p. 103. (VII² B 235, p. 137).

CHAPTER 7. REVELATION AND RELIGIOUS AUTHORITY

1. A. P. Adler, *Nogle Prædikener* (Copenhagen, 1843).

2. *OAR*, p. 69 (VII² B 235, p. 94).

3. Ibid., p. 71 (VII² B 235, p. 95).

4. A. P. Adler, *Studier* (Copenhagen, 1843).

5. *OAR*, p. 72 (VII² B 235, p. 98).

6. Ibid., p. 76 (VII² B 235, p. 104).

7. August 26, 1845.

8. The receipt from Reitzel's bookshop, dated June 12, 1846, shows that he bought one volume of poems, *Nogle Digte*, and three religious works: *Studier og*

Eksempler, Theologiske Studier, and *Forsog til en kort systematisk Fremstilling af Christendommen i dens Logik.*

9. *Skrivelser min Suspension og Entledigelse vedkommende.* Kierkegaard purchased this book from Reitzel's on August 12, 1846.

10. For more on this point, see Julia Watkin's introduction to *Nutidens Religieuse Forvirring: Bogen om Adler* (Copenhagen: C.A. Reitzels Forlag, 1984), pp. 15–16.

11. This was one of two essays published under the title *Two Minor Ethico-Religious Treatises* (1849), which Kierkegaard attributed to the pseudonym H.H.

12. Robert C. Solomon, *In the Spirit of Hegel: A Study of G. W. F. Hegel's Phenomenology of Spirit* (New York: Oxford University Press, 1983), p. 587.

13. Ibid., p. 586. Of course, we now know that Hegel's mature writings were preceded by a series of unpublished theological manuscripts (1793–1799), in which he took a strongly anti-Christian position. Many of these documents have been published in *Hegel's Early Theological Manuscripts,* translated by T.M. Knox (Chicago: University of Chicago Press, 1948), which contains selections from Hermann Nohl's 1907 edition. Also of interest are the essay fragments contained in *Three Essays 1793–1795,* edited and translated by P. Fuss and J. Dobbins (Notre Dame, IN: University of Notre Dame Press, 1984). For a fuller discussion of the relation between these writings and Hegel's later systematic thought, the reader may consult Stephen Crites, *In the Twilight of Christendom,* pp. 35–57, and Robert C. Solomon, *In the Spirit of Hegel,* pp. 580–634.

14. *CUP,* p. 200 (*SV* VII, p. 187).

15. *SKJP,* vol. 2, p. 226 (X⁴ A 429).

16. Ibid., p. xix (VIII² B 27, p. 79).

17. *SKJP,* vol. 1, p. 108 (IX A 32).

18. *OAR,* p. xvi (VIII² B 27, p. 76).

19. Ronald Hustwit, "Adler and the Ethical: A Study of Kierkegaard's *On Authority and Revelation,*" *Religious Studies* 21 (1985): 338.

20. *OAR,* p. 92 (VII² B 257, p. 291).

21. *AN,* p. 35 X⁵ B 107, p. 290).

22. *CUP,* pp. 200–201 (*SV* VII, pp. 187–188).

23. *OAR,* p. li.

24. Ibid., p. 170 (VII² B 235, pp. 207–208).

25. Ibid., p. 118 (*SV* XI, p. 107).

26. Ibid., p. 24 (VIII² B 13, p. 63).

27. Ibid., p. 111 (VII² B 235, p. 144).

28. Ibid., p. 105 (VII² B 235, p. 138).

29. Ibid.

30. Ibid., p. 87 (VII² B 235, p. 117).

31. Ibid., p. 77 (VII² B 235, p. 105).

32. Ibid., p. 164 (VII² B 235, p. 201).

33. Ibid., p. 165 (VII² B 235, p. 201).

34. Ibid.

35. Ibid., pp. 169–170 (VII2 B 235, p. 206).

36. Ibid., p. 145 (VII² B 235, p. 179).

37. Ibid., p. 86 (VII² B 235, p. 117).

38. Ibid., pp. 92–93 (VII² B 235, p. 127).

39. Ibid., p. 111 (VII² B 235, p. 144).

40. Ibid., pp. 111–112 (VII² B 235, pp. 144–145).

41. Ibid., p. 105 (VII² B 235, p. 138).

42. Ibid., p. 106 (VII² B 261, p. 295).

43. Ibid., p. 107 VII² B 235, p. 140).

44. Ibid., p. 105 (VII² B 235, p. 138).

45. Ibid., p. 106 (VII² B 235, p. 139).

46. Ibid., p. 107 (VII² B 235, p. 140).

47. This example is developed by Hustwit in "Adler and the Ethical," p. 334.

48. *OAR*, p. 110 (VII² B 235, p. 143).

49. Ibid.

50. Ibid., p. 113 (VII² B 235, p. 146).

51. Ibid., p. 117 (VII² B 235, p. 150).

52. Ibid., p. 109 (VII² B 235, p. 142).

53. Ibid., p. 117 (VII² B 235, p. 150).

54. Ibid., p. 110 (VII^2 B 235, p. 143).

55. Ibid., p. 108 (VII^2 B 235, pp. 140–141).

56. R. B. Harris, "The Function and Limits of Religious Authority," in *Authority: A Philosophical Analysis*, edited by R. B. Harris (University: University of Alabama Press, 1976), p. 139.

57. T.H. Croxall, "Kierkegaard on 'Authority,'" *Hibbert Journal* 48 (1949–1950): 151.

58. *SKJP*, vol. 1, p. 75 (X^2 A 119).

59. *Papirer*, V A 32 (trans. T. H. Croxall, "Kierkegaard on 'Authority,'" p. 151).

60. Julia Watkin, ed., *Nutidens Religieuse Forvirring*, by Søren Kierkegaard (Copenhagen: C. A. Reitzels Forlag, 1984), pp. 18–23.

61. *SKJP*, vol. 1, pp. 97–98 (VII^1 B 13).

62. *OAR*, p. 51 (VII^2 B 235, pp. 64–65).

63. Watkin, p. 23.

64. *OAR*, p. 178 (VII^2 B 235, pp. 218–219).

65. Ibid., p. 170 (VII^2 B 235, pp. 208–209).

CHAPTER 8. THE DIALECTIC OF RELIGIOUS COMMUNICATION

1. *SKJP*, vol. 1, pp. 267–308 (VIII^2 B 81–89, pp. 143–190).

2. *SKJP*, vol. 1, p. 270 (VIII^2 B 81).

3. Ibid.

4. Ibid.

5. *CUP*, pp. 176–177 (*SV* VII, p. 183).

6. *EO*, vol. 2, p. 258 (*SV* II, p. 232).

7. *CUP*, pp. 302–303 (*SV* VII, p. 293).

8. Ibid., p. 309 (*SV* VII, p. 300).

9. Ibid., p. 320 (*SV* VII, p. 311).

10. *SKJP*, vol. 2, p. 97 (VII^1 A 139).

11. *CUP*, p. 355 (*SV* VII, p. 344).

12. Ibid., p. 382 (*SV* VII, p. 370).

13. *SKJP*, vol. 1, p. 203 (X¹ A 558).

14. *AN*, p. 36 (X⁵ B 107, p. 291).

15. *CUP*, p. 353 (*SV* VII, p. 342).

16. Ibid., p. 353 (*SV* VII, p. 341).

17. Ibid., p. 355 (*SV* VII, p. 344).

18. Ibid., p. 356 (*SV* VII, p. 344).

19. Ibid.

20. Ibid., p. 70n. (*SV* VII, p. 59n.).

21. *SKJP*, vol. 1, p. 272 (VIII² B 81).

22. Ibid., vol. 1 p. 268 (VIII² B 81).

23. Ibid., vol. 1, p. 271 (VIII² B 81).

24. Ibid., vol. 1, p. 269 (VIII² B 81).

25. Ibid., vol. 1, p. 281 (VIII² B 83).

26. Ibid., vol 1, p. 273 (VIII² B 81).

27. Walter Lowrie, trans., *Training in Christianity*, by Søren Kierkegaard (Princeton: Princeton University Press, 1944), p. 132n.

28. *SKJP*, vol. 1, p. 306 (VIII² B 89).

29. *CUP*, p. 346 (*SV* VII, p. 335).

30. *PC*, p. 134 (*SV* XII, p. 125).

31. Ibid., p. 125–126 (*SV* XII, p. 118).

32. Ibid., p. 127 (*SV* XII, p. 119). Cf. *SKJP*, vol. 1, p. 316 (X² A 367).

33. *CUP*, p. 339 (*SV* VII, pp. 328–329). Cf. *SKJP*, vol. 1, p. 316 (X² A 146).

34. Ibid., p. 192 (*SV* VII, p. 189).

35. Ibid., p. 332n. (*SV* VII, p. 322n.).

36. John A. Mourant, "The Limitations of Religious Existentialism," *International Philosophical Quarterly* 1 (1961): 437–452.

37. Ibid., pp. 437–438.

38. *CUP*, p. 182 (*SV* VII, p. 170).

39. Ibid., p. 68n. (*SV* VII, pp. 56–57n.).

40. Mourant, pp. 441–442.

41. Ibid., p. 444.

42. *AN*, p. 42 (X⁵ B 107, p. 297).

43. See Walter Lowrie, *Kierkegaard*, vol. 1, p. 275.

44. Mourant, p. 444.

45. *SKJP*, vol. 1, p. 203 (X¹ A 558).

46. Ibid., vol. 1, p. 274 (VIII² B 81).

47. *PC*, p. 134 (*SV* XII, p. 125).

48. Mourant, p. 448.

49. *CUP*, p. 180 (*SV* VII, p. 168).

50. Paul L. Holmer, "Kierkegaard and the Sermon," *Journal of Religion* 37 (1957): 7.

51. Ibid.

52. *AN*, p. 46 (X⁵ B 107, p. 301).

53. Ibid., p. 35 (X⁵ B 107, p. 29.

54. Ibid., p. 42 (X⁵ B 107, p. 297).

55. Ibid.

56. *PV*, p. 37 (*SV* XIII, p. 539).

57. Harry S. Broudy, "Kierkegaard on Indirect Communication," *Journal of Philosophy* 55 (1961): 225.

58. *PV*, p. 24 (*SV* XIII, p. 531). In the note to this passage, Kierkegaard writes: "One may recall the *Concluding Postscript*, the author of which, Johannes Climacus, declares expressly that he himself is not a Christian."

CONCLUDING REMARKS

1. Karl Barth, *Doctrine of the Word of God* (Edinburgh: T&T Clark, 1936), p. 350.

2. Brand Blanshard, *Reason and Belief* (New Haven: Yale University Press, 1975), p. 34.

Selected Bibliography

A. *Works by Kierkegaard*

Kierkegaard, S. *Either/Or* (1843). 2 vols. Edited and translated by Howard V. Hong and Edna H. Hong. Princeton: Princeton University Press, 1987.

——. *Philosophical Fragments* (1844). Edited and translated by Howard V. Hong and Edna H. Hong. Princeton: Princeton University Press, 1985.

——. *The Concept of Anxiety* (1844). Translated by Reidar Thomte in collaboration with Albert B. Anderson. Princeton: Princeton University Press, 1980.

——. *Concluding Unscientific Postscript* (1846). Translated by David F. Swenson and Walter Lowrie. Princeton: Princeton University Press, 1941.

——. *Two Ages: A Literary Review* (1846). Edited and translated by Howard V. Hong and Edna H. Hong. Princeton: Princeton University Press, 1978.

——. *On Authority and Revelation: The Book on Adler* (1846–47). Translated by Walter Lowrie. New York: Harper & Row, 1966.

——. *Armed Neutrality* (1848–49). In *Armed Neutrality* and *An Open Letter*. Translated by Howard V. Hong and Edna H. Hong. Bloomington: Indiana University Press, 1968.

——. *The Sickness Unto Death* (1849). Edited and translated by Howard V. Hong and Edna H. Hong. Princeton: Princeton University Press, 1980.

——. *Practice in Christianity* (1850). Edited and translated by Howard V. Hong and Edna H. Hong. Princeton: Princeton University Press, 1991.

——. *The Point of View for My Work as an Author* (1859). Translated by Walter Lowrie. New York: Harper & Row, 1962.

——. *Eighteen Upbuilding Discourses.* Edited and translated by Howard V. Hong and Edna H. Hong. Princeton: Princeton University Press, 1990.

——. *The Corsair Affair.* Edited and translated by Howard V. Hong and Edna H. Hong. Princeton: Princeton University Press, 1982.

——. *Søren Kierkegaard's Journals and Papers.* 7 vols. Edited and translated by Howard V. Hong and Edna H. Hong, assisted by Gregor Malantschuk. Bloomington: Indiana University Press, 1967–1978.

B. Books about Kierkegaard

Barrett, William. *Irrational Man.* New York: Doubleday, 1962.

Bohlin, Torsten. *Kierkegaards Tro och Andra Kierkegaard Studier.* Stockholm: Svenska Kyrkans Diakonistyrelsens Bokförlag, 1944.

Brøchner, Hans. *Erindringer om Kierkegaard.* Edited with an introduction and notes by Steen Johansen. Copenhagen, 1953.

Caputo, John D. *Radical Hermeneutics.* Bloomington: Indiana University Press, 1987.

Collins, James. *The Mind of Kierkegaard.* Princeton: Princeton University Press, 1983.

Crites, Stephen. *In the Twilight of Christendom: Hegel vs. Kierkegaard on Faith and History.* Chambersburg, PA: American Academy of Religion, 1972.

Diem, Hermann. *Kierkegaard: An Introduction.* Translated by David Green. Richmond: John Knox Press, 1966.

Evans, C. Stephen. *Kierkegaard's "Fragments" and "Postscript": The Religious Philosophy of Johannes Climacus.* Atlantic Highlands, NJ: Humanities Press, 1983.

——. *Passionate Reason: Making Sense of Kierkegaard's Philosophical Fragments.* Bloomington: Indiana University Press, 1992.

Fenger, Henning. *Kierkegaard, The Myths and Their Origins: Studies in the Kierkegaardian Papers and Letters.* Translated by George C. Schoolfield. New Haven: Yale University Press, 1976.

Ferreira, M. Jamie. *Transforming Vision: Imagination and Will in Kierkegaardian Faith.* Oxford: The Clarendon Press, 1991.

Garelick, Herbert M. *The Anti-Christianity of Kierkegaard.* The Hague: Martinus Nijhoff, 1965.

Green, Ronald M. *Kierkegaard and Kant: The Hidden Debt.* Albany: State University of New York Press, 1992.

Johnson, H. and Niels Thulstrup, eds. *A Kierkegaard Critique.* New York: Harper & Row, 1962.

Kirmmse, Bruce H. *Kierkegaard in Golden Age Denmark.* Bloomington: Indiana University Press, 1990.

Lowrie, Walter. *Kierkegaard.* 2 vols. New York: Harper & Brothers, 1962.

Mackey, Louis. *Points of View: Readings of Kierkegaard.* Tallahasse: The Florida State University Press, 1986.

Müller, Paul. *Meddelelsensdialektik i Søren Kierkegaards Philosophiske Smuler.* Copenhagen: C.A. Reitzel, 1979.

Pojman, Louis P. *The Logic of Subjectivity.* University: University of Alabama Press, 1984.

Taylor, Mark C. *Kierkegaard's Pseudonymous Authorship: A Study of Time and the Self.* Princeton: Princeton University Press, 1975.

——. *Journeys to Selfhood: Hegel and Kierkegaard.* Berkeley and Los Angeles: University of California Press, 1980.

Thomas, J. Heywood. *Subjectivity and Paradox.* London: Oxford University Press, 1957.

Thulstrup, Niels. *Kierkegaards forhold til Hegel of til den spekulative Idealisme indtil 1846.* Copenhagen: Gyldendal, 1967.

Watkin, Julia, ed. *Nutidens Religieuse Forvirring,* by S. Kierkegaard. Copenhagen: C.A. Reitzels Forlag, 1984.

C. Articles about Kierkegaard

Adams, Robert. "Kierkegaard's Arguments Against Objective Reasoning in Religion." *Monist* 60 (1977): 228–243.

Allison, Henry E. "Christianity and Nonsense." *Review of Metaphysics* 20 (1966–67): 432–460.

Blanshard, Brand. "Kierkegaard on Faith." *Personalist* 49 (1968): 5–23.

Broudy, Harry S. "Kierkegaard on Indirect Communication." *Journal of Philosophy* 58 (1961): 225–233.

180   Kierkegaard and the Concept of Revelation

Cavell, Stanley. "Kierkegaard's 'On Authority and Revelation.'" In *Must We Mean What We Say?* New York: Cambridge University Press, 1976, pp. 163–179.

Croxall, T. H. "Kierkegaard on 'Authority.'" *Hibbert Journal* 48 (1949–50): 145–152.

Evans, C. Stephen. "Is Kierkegaard an Irrationalist? Reason, Paradox, and Faith." *Religious Studies* 25 (1989): 347–362.

———. "The Relevance of Historical Evidence for Christian Faith: A Critique of a Kierkegaardian View." *Faith and Philosophy* 7 (1990): 470–485.

———. "Does Kierkegaard Think Beliefs Can be Directly Willed?" *International Journal for Philosophy of Religion* 26 (1989): 173–184.

Ferreira, M. Jamie. "Kierkegaardian Faith: 'the Condition' and 'the Response.'" *International Journal for Philosophy of Religion* 28 (1990): 63–79.

———. "Seeing (Just) IS Believing: Faith and Imagination." *Faith and Philosophy* 9 (1992): 151–167.

Holmer, Paul. "Kierkegaard and Ethical Theory." *Ethics* 63 (1953): 157–170.

———. "Kierkegaard and Logic." *Kierkegaardiana* 2 (1957): 25–42.

———. "Kierkegaard and the Sermon." *Journal of Religion* 37 (1957): 1–9.

Hustwit, Ronald. "Adler and the Ethical: A Study of Kierkegaard's *On Authority and Revelation.*" *Religious Studies* 21 (1985): 331–348.

Mourant, J. A. "The Limitations of Religious Existentialism." *International Philosophical Quarterly* 1 (1961): 437–452.

Pedersen, Bertel. "Fictionality and Authority: A Point of View for Kierkegaard's Work as an Author." In *Kierkegaard.* Ed. Harold Bloom. New York: Chelsea House Publishers, 1989, pp. 99–115.

Stengren, George. "Faith." *Kierkegaardiana* 12 (1982): 83–92.

Wisdo, David. "Kierkegaard on Belief, Faith, and Explanation." *International Journal for Philosophy of Religion* 21 (1987): 95–114.

D. Other Works Consulted

Dunning, Stephen N. *Kierkegaard's Dialectic of Inwardness: A Structural Analysis of the Theory of Stages.* Princeton: Princeton University Press, 1985.

Geismar, Eduard. *Søren Kierkegaard: Hans Livsudvikling og Forfattervirksomhed.* 2 vols. Copenhagen: G. E. C. Gad, 1927–1928.

Himmelstrup, Jens. *Søren Kierkegaard: International Bibliography.* Copenhagen: Nyt Nordisk Forlag, 1962.

Holm, Søren. *Søren Kierkegaards Historiefilosofi.* Copenhagen: Nyt Nordisk Forlag, 1952.

Høffding, Harald. *Søren Kierkegaard som Filosof.* Copenhagen: P. G. Philipsens Forlag, 1892.

Jørgensen, Aage. *Søren Kierkegaard-Litteratur, 1961–1970.* Aarhus: Akademisk Boghandel, 1971.

Koch, C. H. *En flue paa Hegels udødelige Næse, eller om Adolph Peter Adler og om Søren Kierkegaards forhold til ham* (Copenhagen: C.A. Reitzels Forlag, 1991).

Malantschuk, Gregor. *Kierkegaard's Thought.* Edited and translated by Howard V. Hong and Edna H. Hong. Princeton: Princeton University Press, 1971.

Rhode, H. P., ed. *Auktions protokol over Søren Kierkegaards Bogsamling.* Copenhagen, 1967.

Tennemann, W. G. *Geschichte der Philosophie.* 11 vols. Leipzig, 1798–1819.

Thulstrup, Niels, ed. *Breve og Aktstykker vedrørende Søren Kierkegaard.* Copenhagen, 1953.

Trendelenburg, Adolph. *Logische Untersuchungen.* Berlin, 1840.

Index